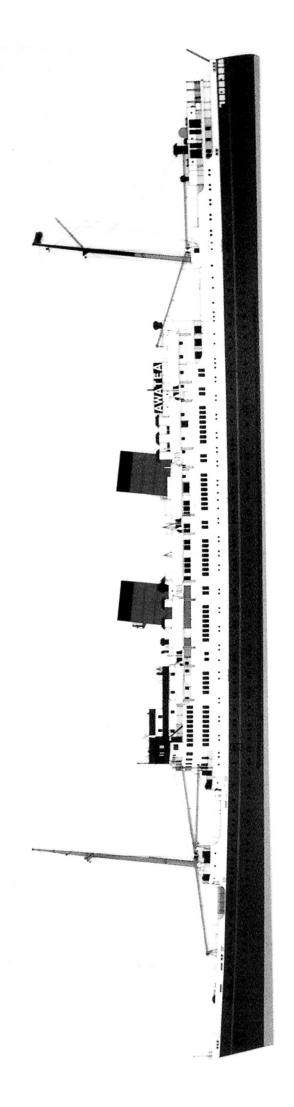

Awatea. [Murray Robinson]

A TASMAN TRIO

Wanganella – Awatea – Monowai

Andrew Bell and Murray Robinson

Ships in Focus Publications

Published in the UK in 2009 by Ships in Focus Publications,
18 Franklands, Longton
Preston PR4 5PD
ISBN 978-1-901703-55-9

Front cover: The *Wanganella* at Belfast newly renamed, refitted and repainted for Huddart Parker. *[Newall Dunn collection]*
Above: The Huddart Parker liner *Wanganella* at Auckland in February 1938. *[Ian J. Farquhar collection]*
Back cover top: The *Wanganella* at Wellington in the funnel colours of McIlwraith McEacharn Ltd.
Middle: The final sailing; *Monowai* dressed overall as she leaves Wellington in 1960 for her last Tasman crossing.
Bottom: Queen's Wharf, Wellington with the *Monowai* about to depart. *[All: V. H. Young and L. A. Sawyer]*

The *Monowai* berthed at Central Wharf, Auckland during the late 1950s. *[Alexander Turnbull Library, Wellington, New Zealand. National Publicity Studios Collection, F29986 1/2]*

FOREWORD

In a world that has become used to being able to travel between even the remotest places in 48 hours it is easily forgotten how, in living memory, passenger ships were the accepted, often the only, way to travel. This book tells the stories of three ships which sustained and were the last to regularly link two Commonwealth countries, Australia and New Zealand. When they were placed in a sector of what was quaintly called the 'All Red (British Empire) Route' in the early 1930s, both the Federation of Australia's six states and the Dominion of New Zealand had small populations (Australia 6.5 million, and New Zealand 1.6 million), their economies were small and yet to be developed, and their potential had been stultified by a world recession of unparalleled severity. It was only a privileged few who considered travel as part of their regular lives and, beyond them, down aft and on lower decks were those searching for better lives as economic migrants.

A common feature of the histories of the *Wanganella* and *Monowai* was that they were designed and built for trade routes on which they never served, in the former ship's case, and only very briefly in the latter's. It always has been an economic and a technical gamble to place a ship shaped and intended for one trade into another. In habitability terms, for instance, those travelling and working on a ship built to be comfortable in a hot climate cannot expect it to be pleasant in a temperate climate with contrasting seasons and sea conditions.

The *Awatea*, by contrast, did not have to be adapted from the dictates of a previous owner. She was built entirely and specifically to meet both the Tasman weather and the competition from bigger, faster, grander ships that, just a few years after they had been acquired, saw the *Wanganella* and the *Monowai* reduced to second place. Immensely successful, the all–conquering *Awatea* might have gone on to even greater renown in the brief but brilliant last blossoming of sea travel in the 1950s and 60s, had she survived the Second World War.

Where the *Wanganella*, the *Monowai* and the *Awatea* markedly diverged was in the choice of their propulsion machinery. P&O's choice of engines for *Razmak*, which became *Monowai*, was long guided by the need for reliability on long-haul routes: steam turbines had been specified in some of their new buildings and with the *Viceroy of India* (19,648/1929) the leap had been made into pioneering turbo-electric power. The *Wanganella* had been ordered by a subsidiary of what was at the time the world's largest

shipping group, Royal Mail, who for economic reasons had embraced the youngest form of propulsion, namely the diesel engine. So committed were they to motor ships that they were being built for every company's fleet in the group. In 1927 plans were even well advanced for a 1,000-foot long liner for White Star that was to be powered by diesel-electric propulsion, exactly the same system that, in her 1987 conversion, saved the *Queen Elizabeth 2* from early oblivion. Choice of engines for the *Awatea* was determined by one single factor: speed. She had to cross the Tasman Sea in two and a half days, which required a minimum speed of 20 knots with more to spare, and she had to have engines free from noise, vibration and high costs. Diesels were first considered, but steam turbines were the answer.

Another common theme was that the owners of all three ships were headed by dominant personalities. As the *Razmak*, the *Monowai* came into service when James Mackay, the first Earl of Inchcape (1852-1932), was making his last hurrah: he was a man who had bought the constituent parts of an Empire-wide shipping venture together. For the *Achimota*, the might-have-been- flagship of Elder Dempster, the *Wanganella* was the creation of Owen Philipps, First Baron Kylsant, whose career was soon to end in failure, opprobrium and disgrace. She was to become the longest-lived of his once vast fleet. The *Awatea* was, in turn, the product of another highly gifted maritime leader whose time was also ended suddenly, in his case by fatal ill-health. The New Zealander Norris Stephen Falla became Managing Director of the Union Steam Ship Company as it was losing its grip on the vital Tasman trade and when courage and energy were desperately needed to find the right solution. His *Awatea* was the shortest-lived but by far the most outstanding of all the ships that served the Tasman Sea.

The co-authors were drawn together by a common interest in ships' general arrangement plans. Murray Robinson needed them as a basis for his peerless waterline profile drawings of which Andrew Bell is the proud owner of an original and he is also the custodian of a large collection of plans. They have jointly written a history of three ships from an era when cables were almost the only form of telecommunication, and done it at a time when the instantaneous e-mail network links Murray on the shores of the Tasman Sea and Andrew on the coastline of the Atlantic in Cornwall.

John Clarkson   Roy Fenton

INTRODUCTION

With her straight stem and squat, flat-topped funnels below tall, raked masts, the *Wanganella* of 1932 had the classic profile of a Pirrie-Kylsant motor liner. At 9,576 tons she was not among the largest or most prestigious of her contemporaries, but of all of them she perhaps had the most remarkable career, lasting until 1970. She spent nearly all her life on the opposite side of the world to the service for which she was built. In New Zealand the name *Wanganella* has become part of local folklore. She is the 'Wanga' of Deep Cove, moored there as an accommodation ship for six and a half years, and she is 'Wanganella Weather', from the time in 1947 when the winds and seas amazingly stayed calm for 18 days while she lay impaled on Barrett Reef.

The spark for this book came from an e-mail conversation in February 2006 between the authors, one of us in Cornwall, the other in New Zealand. We were reflecting on the diverse and truly fascinating life the *Wanganella* led. Not for her the usual 20 to 25 years plying back and forth on her owner's trade routes, to then pass into obscurity in some faraway scrap yard. Instead, she went from one career to the next evading war hazards, shipwreck and the perils of commerce. At the age of more than 40 years she was scrapped only because her engines had given out. Yet not a lot has been written about the *Wanganella*. Initially we began work on an article for publication in Ships in Focus 'Record', but so much material came our way that the article has become a book.

Regular travellers on the Tasman crossing during the 1950s were sure of one thing: they *always* booked on 'their' *Wanganella*. But just as stalwart were the many passengers who remained loyal to the other ship that shared the Tasman service in those post-war, pre-airliner years. She was the *Monowai* of the Union Steam Ship Company of New Zealand Ltd. No reminiscence of voyaging the Tasman Sea during those far-gone times would be complete without the *Monowai*. The *Wanganella* and the *Monowai* were twin-screw, twin-funnel vessels launched within a few years of each other by the same shipbuilder, intended for trade routes far removed from where they spent their working lives. Both were fine ships with distinguished war records and they enjoyed great commercial success, becoming very well-known and very well-liked. Fate intervened at a crucial time for both ships when they were at the beginning of their careers, saving them from years of lay up and uselessness. Both sailed into great old age and ended their lives in Far Eastern scrapyards. But there the similarity ended. The *Wanganella* was a motor ship with, in 1931, the latest diesel technology. The *Monowai* had old-fashioned steam reciprocating engines yet she was five knots faster. The *Wanganella* had the squat-funnel, cruiser stern, square upright superstructure of the Pirrie-Kylsant ships; the *Monowai* completed just six years earlier had a much lower, classic profile with tall raked funnels and a beautiful counter stern.

Certainly the *Monowai* and perhaps even the *Wanganella* would not have been kept by their respective owners after the end of the Second World War had the third ship featured in this book, the *Awatea*, not been lost during the 1939-45 conflict. She was a quite exceptional ship: with all six boilers lit her turbines could drive her at a spectacular 26 knots as opposed to the *Wanganella's* lumbering 14 knots and the *Monowai's* more respectable 19 knots. Everything about the *Awatea* was consummate: her record-breaking speed, her legendary captain, her beautiful looks and her magnificent interiors. Hers was a life of great triumph and heroic tragedy, for the *Awatea* features in our story for just six years before her destruction during the fighting of 1942. The Royal Navy officer commanding the seaborne invasion in which the *Awatea* was lost famously wrote that she 'fought the battle of a battleship'.

Perhaps some older generation passengers, travelling at 30,000 feet on the airliners that daily cross the Tasman, might look down at the sea far below and remember the days when their two-hour flight was, instead, three and a half leisurely or seasick days aboard the *Wanganella* or the *Monowai*. This book is in memory of both these ships and of the mighty *Awatea*.

Andrew Bell
Porthleven
Cornwall
England

Murray Robinson
Raumati Beach
Kapiti Coast
New Zealand

April 2009

CONTENTS

SOURCES AND ACKNOWLEDGEMENTS

Scrapbooks of 'The Evening Post' and 'The Dominion' newspaper clippings, kindly provided to the authors by John and Jenny Dallow of Auckland, New Zealand.
Newspaper clippings on the careers of *Wanganella* and *Monowai*, kindly provided to the authors by Ian Farquhar of Dunedin, New Zealand.
'A History of Union Steamship Co. of New Zealand' by A.L. Arbon.
'Across the Sea to War' by Peter Plowman.
Alexander Turnbull Library, National Library of New Zealand.
'Australia in the War of 1939-1945. Royal Australian Navy 1942-1945' by G. Herman Gill.
'Australian Coastal Shipping' by Barry Pemberton.
Bill Laxon Library, New Zealand National Maritime Museum.
'BI The British India Steam Navigation Company Limited' by W.A. Laxon and F.W. Perry.
'Canterbury Coasters' by Gavin McLean.
'A Century of Style' by N.H. Brewer.
'Civil Aviation in New Zealand' by David Rendel.
'Cook Strait Ferries (As I knew Them)' by R.D. Munro.
'Davey and the Awatea' by W.A. Laxon.
'Evening Post' photo archive, National Library of New Zealand.
'Famous Ships Belfast Built' by Laurence Dunn.
'Fifty Years Ago - The Stranding of the Wanganella' by Max Hodgson in 'New Zealand Marine News' Volume 46, No. 2, 1997.
'Flightpath South Pacific' by Ian H. Driscoll.
'Glamour Ships of the Union Steam Ship Company' by J. Churchouse.
'Gold Wings and Webbed Feet' by Don Nairn.
'Hospital Ships' by R. Goodmor.
'Making Waves' by Les Hutchins.
'McIlwraith McEacharn Ltd.' unpublished history by T.S. Stevens.
'New Zealand Naval Vessels' by R.J. McDougall.
'New Zealand Pilot'.
'New Zealand Shipwrecks' by C.W.N. Ingram.
'Niagara's Gold' by Jeff Maynard.
'Passenger Liners' by Laurence Dunn.
'Passenger Ships of Australia and New Zealand' Volume 2, by Peter Plowman.
Radio New Zealand Sound Archives: 'Selwyn Toogood Reports for 2ZB from Beacon Hill.' Interviews with the *Wanganella's* Chief Engineer J. Wylie and D.E. Eadie, Huddart Parker's Marine Engineering Superintendent; 'From the Back Country' interview with Harold Clarke, *Wanganella's* postmaster at Deep Cove.
'Shipbuilders to the World' by M. Moss and J.R. Hume.
'Shipbuilding and Shipping Record'.
'Shipbuilding Ship Repair and Services' Sydney, Australia, July 1948.
'Ships and Sailormen' by A.A. Kirk.

'Ships of Wellington' by Vic Young.
'Spoils from the Sea' by James Taylor.
'The Elder Dempster Fleet History 1852-1985' by James E. Cowden and John O.C. Duffy.
'The Era of Coastal Shipping in New Zealand - the Small Motor Ships' by Murray Jennings.
'The Heart of Fiordland' by George A. Howard.
'The History of New Zealand Aviation' by Ross Ewing and Ross MacPherson.
'The Line that Dared' edited by Gordon McLauchlan.
'The Trade Makers' by Peter Davies.
'The Tyser Legacy' by Ian Farquhar.
'The Vanished Fleet' by T.K. Fitchett.
'Union Fleet' by Ian Farquhar.
'War Service of the Merchant Navy: A Record of the Participation of the Men and Ships of Huddart Parker Ltd.' kindly provided to the authors by Ian Farquhar.
'Warships of the Imperial Japanese Navy, 1869-1945' by Hansgeorg Jentschura, Dieter Jung and Peter Mickel.
'Wayfarer and Warrior The Monowai Story' by Jack Harker.
'Wellington Harbour' by David Johnson.
'Where Giants Dwell' by Gerry Evans.
'Wings Across the Tasman' by Leslie Jillett.

The authors would first like to thank John Clarkson and Roy Fenton of Ships in Focus Publications. Ian Farquhar of Dunedin, New Zealand was of immense help providing us with information from his extensive files. John and Jenny Dallow of Auckland, New Zealand very kindly loaned the authors their two scrapbooks of original newspaper clippings recording the *Wanganella's* 1947-48 stranding and repairs. Ken Bradley of Te Anau, New Zealand helped us with advice on where to find information about the *Wanganella's* time at Deep Cove.

    For assistance with photos we are most grateful to:
Vic Young of Wellington, New Zealand; Ian Farquhar; John and Marion Clarkson; Peter Newall; the Alexander Turnbull Library, Archives New Zealand and the Wellington City Archives of Wellington New Zealand; Iain Lovie of Napier, New Zealand; the Ulster Folk and Transport Museum; the Vickers Photographic Archive at the Dock Museum, Barrow-in-Furness; Ken Bradley and Morag Forrester of Fiordland Museum in Te Anau, New Zealand; Dean Miller and Wendy Adlam of the Wellington Museum of City and Sea, New Zealand; and Marleene Boyd of the Bill Laxon Maritime Library, New Zealand National Maritime Museum, Auckland. Lastly but never least, we acknowledge and thank our respective wives Prue Bell and Louise Robinson for their assistance with proof reading and typing.

The *Wanganella* aground on Barrett Reef, Wellington Harbour in January 1947. *[Authors' collection]*

WANGANELLA - FROM WEST AFRICA TO DEEP COVE

The *Achimota*

Few ships that went on to achieve long, lucky and successful careers have had a more inauspicious start than the *Wanganella*. Originally intended to be the flagship of one owner's fleet, she became that of another's in a different hemisphere. Of all the British shipping companies that provided the seaborne trade sinews of Empire in the 1920s, none needed the technological development offered by the diesel engine more than Elder Dempster and its service to West Africa. Anything that increased cargo carrying capacity on a draught limited to around 22 feet (6.7 metres) over coastal river shallows, while reducing the need to carry a large amount of Welsh steam coal was worth putting capital into, even a pioneering type of propulsion. So it was no coincidence that Elder Dempster's 7,937 ton *Aba* was, in 1920, the world's first diesel-engined passenger ship. She was joined in 1922 by *Adda*. With these two liners successfully participating in the sailings scheduled weekly from Liverpool to West Africa, two more ships were ordered from Harland and Wolff, *Accra* being completed in August 1926 and then *Apapa* in January 1927.

The missionaries behind the practical implementation of the concept for these diesel-powered ships were William Pirrie (1847-1924), the first Viscount, and Owen Cosby Philipps (1863-1937), created First Baron Kylsant in 1923. One was Chairman and Managing Director of Harland and Wolff Ltd., the world's leading shipbuilder and the other headed the Royal Mail Group, Britain's largest shipping conglomerate. Each man impressed the other. In 1909 the two had joined interests to swiftly buy Elder Dempster from the estate of Sir Alfred Jones who had, over 30 years, established the company in an unrivalled position dominating West African shipping both ashore and afloat.

It was a natural progression for Elder Dempster to order, in May 1928, a fifth diesel-engined passenger ship from its partners in Belfast. Yard No. 849 was of almost identical design to *Accra* and *Apapa* but with a slightly larger hull, more powerful main engines and, following the fashion of the time, two funnels of which the forward one was a dummy. At 9,576 gross register tonnage and 5,625 tons net, she was to have a length overall of 479 feet, a breadth of 63 feet 6 inches and a draught fully loaded of 24 feet 6 inches. (Figures as published in 'Shipbuilding and Shipping Record' of 15th December 1932. Figures in other publications vary.) The ship's hull would be divided into eight watertight compartments with seven bulkheads. Accommodation was to be for 236 first and 64 second class passengers plus an unspecified number of third class and African native deck passengers. Four holds

Owen Cosby Philipps
Lord Kylsant

Sir Owen Cosby Philipps KCMG GCMG was the first and last Baron Kylsant of Carmarthen and of Amroth, and Chairman of the Royal Mail Group, also known as the Kylsant Group. This was a vast amalgam of shipping companies established by Lord Kylsant that included Elder Dempster, for whom the *Achimota* was built.

Of Welsh ancestry, Lord Kylsant was born on 25th March 1863 and as a young man went into business as a tramp ship owner. He become Chairman and Managing Director of the Royal Mail Steam Packet Company in 1903 and during the next 28 years he expanded Royal Mail into the biggest combine of shipping interests in the world, employing nearly 60,000 people. Most notable amongst its holdings were the Union-Castle Line, acquired in 1912, and White Star Line, acquired in 1927. Elder Dempster and Co. Ltd. was taken over in 1909.

Lord Kylsant believed strongly that times of economic recession, such as the early 1920s, would soon be followed by prosperity as the cycle of boom and bust followed its normal course. He therefore pressed ahead with expansion

and borrowings on a huge scale, paying £7 million for White Star in 1927. But instead of leading to a resurgence in trade, the 1920s slump morphed into the Great Depression of the early 1930s. Mounting losses were cleverly disguised in financial statements put out by Kylsant but in 1930, no longer able to borrow to repay debt, he fell behind with repayments to White Star's former owners. Growing unease about the true state of the finances of the Royal Mail Group led to the British Government setting up a committee of investigation. This in turn resulted in Lord Kylsant being prosecuted at the Old Bailey in 1931 on charges of misleading his directors and investors with false accounts. He was imprisoned for 12 months, was stripped of his knighthoods, and the whole financial merry-go-round of the Royal Mail Group fell apart. Years of work by receivers were needed to sort out the resulting mess, with losses to shareholders and creditors amounting to £50 million, a colossal figure in those times. After his release Lord Kylsant lived in obscurity at his home in Wales, dying there on 25th June 1937 aged 74. He had no male heir, and so his title lapsed upon his death.

Although he was disgraced, the legacy of Owen Cosby Philipps is the series of superb passengers liners known today as the Pirrie-Kylsant motor ships. The *Achimota*, soon-to-be *Wanganella*, was one of them. Characterised by their broad, squat funnels, these ships were powered by diesel machinery instead of the usual steam engines. Liners such as White Star's *Georgic* and *Britannic*, Union-Castle's *Carnarvon Castle* and the magnificent *Asturias* and *Alcantara*, built for Royal Mail, rank among the finest ships from the golden era of sea travel before and after the Second World War.

The origins of the *Achimota's* design are clearly evident in these two views of her immediate predecessors: Elder Dempster's *Adda* of 1922 (above) and *Accra* of 1926 (below). Both liners were, like the *Achimota*, products of Harland and Wolff and both were motor ships. Elder Dempster had the distinction of commissioning the world's very first passenger liner powered by diesels: the 7,937 gross register tonnage motor ship *Aba* of 1920. She was so successful on her owner's trade routes to the shallow-draught ports of West Africa that Elder Dempster immediately ordered the 7,816 gross register tonnage *Adda* built at Harland and Wolff's Greenock shipyard. Unlike the *Aba*, *Adda* did not survive the Second World War; she was torpedoed by German submarine *U 107* off Freetown, West Africa on 8th June 1941 with the loss of 12 of her complement. *[B. and A. Feilden/J. and M. Clarkson collection]*

Had a dummy funnel been added atop the *Accra's* bridge house (above) she would have been virtually identical in appearance to the *Achimota*. Of 9,337 gross register tonnage and 28 feet shorter in length than the *Achimota*, the *Accra* was completed for Elder Dempster in August 1926 and was followed in January 1927 by a sister ship, the *Apapa*, also built at Belfast by Harland and Wolff. Along with the *Adda*, the *Accra* and the *Apapa* were lost through enemy action early in the Second World War, the *Accra* being torpedoed by the submarine *U 34* off Rockall in the Outer Hebrides on 26th July 1940 with 19 killed, while the *Apapa* was bombed and sunk south west of Ireland on 15th November the same year with 24 killed. *[B. and A. Feilden/J. and M. Clarkson collection]*

with 265,625 cubic feet of space would enable her to carry approximately 4,000 tons of general cargo.

Engines driving twin screws comprised two sets of Harland-Burmeister and Wain eight-cylinder, single-acting, four-stroke, airless-injection diesels each fitted with turbo-chargers. Their combined output was 8,500 brake horse power at 108 rpm, giving a service speed of 14.5 knots. The cylinders were 740 millimetres in diameter and had a piston stroke of 1,500 millimetres. Three Harland-Burmeister and Wain 250 kW six-cylinder diesel generators, located immediately forward of the main engines in the same compartment, supplied electric power to the ship. An emergency three-cylinder 50kW diesel generator was also fitted, giving the ship a total capacity of 800 kW from all four diesel generators. All the ship's engine room auxiliary machinery together with the steering gear, refrigerating plant, pumps, winches and the windlass were electrically driven. The engines were all manufactured by Harland and Wolff at their Glasgow diesel engine works. In addition, a Clarkson exhaust gas boiler supplied 4,000 pounds of steam per hour at a pressure of 100 psi for the ship's domestic needs. Two oil fuel burners produced the same quantity of steam when the ship was in port. Bunkers for 1,120 tons of marine diesel were provided, with consumption at 30 tons per day for 15 knots. She could also carry some 820 tons of fresh water.

When the order for the new ship was announced in August 1928 it was followed by a further announcement, one month later, that building and commissioning would be as soon as possible with mention being made of a sister ship. The price to build her was approximately £342,500. In April 1929 'The Motor Ship', a crusading monthly trade magazine, reported that there was a delay in completing the main engines. The reason was not given but may have been influenced by Kylsant's acquisition of the White Star Line, the summit of his ambition but putting the whole of the Royal Mail Group under increased financial strain. In August 1929 Yard No. 849 was named *Achimota* after the Gold Coast's - later Ghana's - university college and on 17th December 1929 she was launched. Royal Mail's plight meant the launch took place with neither ceremony nor sponsor. Then, not a week later, the coaster bringing the new ship's two main engines from Glasgow was lost. *Lairdselm* (687/1911, ex *Sable*) put into Loch Ryan while on passage to Belfast when her master became concerned about his ship's stability. His anxiety proved valid; she capsized at 2 am on 22nd December within the shelter of the Loch.

Throughout the 1920s the Royal Mail Group's reported profits had fluctuated between £250,000 and £1,000,000 but in the summer of 1929 the signs became apparent that the Group was disintegrating financially. What was the real value of the fleet? In 1928 the whole Group had earned a net profit of only £457,216 but the fleet was on the books at a total value of £16,200,000. In reality, it was probably worth no more than around £2,500,000. All this was nothing more than the latest display of Kylsant's masterly creative accounting. A reported net profit of £6,000,000 in the period 1921-1929 for the Group was, in truth, a £1,000,000 loss. As details became known in February 1930, Elder Dempster was revealed to have unsecured liabilities of £1,300,000. Publicly owned shares in the Royal Mail Group that had so recently been blue chip were now valueless. The Kylsant Crash was a financial tsunami for British shipping.

With Elder Dempster selling a ship every month on a depressed market to keep operational, there was no chance that *Achimota* could be paid for. Since 1919 the Royal Mail Group had a controlling interest in Harland and Wolff and, as a result, in times of rampant inflation most of the yard's ships were built 'on commission'. By mid-summer of 1931, Frederick Rebbeck (1877-1964), Harland and Wolff's Managing Director, was quoted as saying the 'outlook was atrocious' for there were only three ships left in the yard: *Georgic* (27,759/1932) building for the White Star Line and being paid for by a subvention from the Government of Northern Ireland, Royal Mail's *Highland Patriot* (14,172/1932) and the completed *Achimota*. Under the command of Captain A.H. Crapper she had finally run trials on 2nd July 1931, three years after her keel was laid and after a new set of main engines had been manufactured for her. On her trials the *Achimota* achieved a top speed of 16.7 knots. Immediately following her trials she was laid up at Belfast.

Dated 6th June 1929, this photo looks across part of Harland and Wolff's Queen's Island shipyard at Belfast in Northern Island and shows erection of the *Achimota's* hull to be well advanced, with plating-in almost completed. *[Ulster Folk and Transport Museum, 2488]*

Top left: one of the huge diesel engines in Harland and Wolff's erecting shop at their Finnieston diesel engine works in Glasgow, prior to being shipped to Belfast and lifted aboard the *Achimota*. The size of this machine can be judged by the man in overalls standing at the top of the steps.

Top right: the new ship on launch day. No launch platform has been installed under the bow of the ship from where distinguished guests might observe the traditional naming ceremony surrounded by the usual festive crowd of shipyard workers. As the company for which she was built could not pay the final instalments for her, the *Achimota* was sent down the ways into the River Lagan on 17th December 1929 with nothing to mark the occasion.

Middle right: the *Achimota* entering the water for the very first time. Note the tall davits in place, ready for the ship's lifeboats.

Bottom: The *Achimota* just after she was launched, and with fitting out now to commence. The solitary figures on her forecastle and above her bridge seem to evoke the ship's orphaned, unwanted status. Entangled in the collapse of the Kylsant Group, Elder Dempster could not take delivery of its new liner and so ownership of the *Achimota* reverted to Harland and Wolff, who were now faced with having to complete the ship on their own account and then find a buyer for her. They had to do so while caught in an unprecedented trade slump as the Great Depression took hold. *[Ulster Folk and Transport Museum, 2849, 2844, 2847 and 2848]*

Elder Dempster's loss was Huddart Parker's gain. These two beautiful photographs convey what an impressive ship the *Achimota* was, seen here leaving Belfast in July 1931 for her builder's trials (above) and then running her trials in Belfast Lough (below). Although she was never to be owned by the company, the *Achimota* was completed in Elder Dempster's hull and funnel colours. So bad was the lingering memory of the flagship it was denied, Elder Dempster never again named a ship *Achimota*. Note in the bottom photo how the *Achimota's* varnished teak wheelhouse is set back from the front of the bridge, with two levels of awning spars over the deck space immediately forward of the wheelhouse. This was a practice followed by Elder Dempster and allowed masters and deck officers to be out in the open under the shelter of canvas awnings, while navigating their ships in the equatorial heat and humidity of West Africa. *[Ulster Folk and Transport Museum, 3032 and 3194]*

The *Achimota* brand-new and laid up at Belfast while Harland and Wolff searches for a buyer. It was to here that representatives of Huddart Parker Ltd. of Melbourne, Australia first came in mid-1932 to look over the ship. They would have soon realised they had a bargain for the taking: a liner of the right size for Huddart Parker's needs, ready in all respects for sea, and with financially straitened Harland and Wolff only too willing to offer them a very good price. *[John McRoberts/J. and M. Clarkson collection]*

Huddart Parker

Desperate to find a buyer for the *Achimota*, Frederick Rebbeck must have contacted every owner outside the Royal Mail Group for whom Harland and Wolff had built passenger ships during the past 20 years. Having as recently as 1929 completed the *Westralia* (8,107gt) for Huddart Parker Ltd. of Melbourne, Australia, this was a ship owner that needed no convincing about the advantages of diesel-powered vessels. Established at Geelong on Port Phillip Bay in 1876, Huddart Parker was one of Australia's leading maritime companies. Its venerable twin-screw coal burner *Ulimaroa* (5,777/1908) had operated Huddart Parker's trans-Tasman service between Australia and New Zealand since she was built in 1908, but a replacement ship was now needed that would maintain Huddart Parker's status on this route. Along with the Union Steam Ship Company of New Zealand Ltd. they faced the threat of competition from two fast new liners building for The Oceanic Steamship Company of California, a subsidiary of the Matson Line and due to enter service in 1932. From within the P&O empire of which it was part, the Union Company had in 1930 introduced the *Monowai* (10,852/1925, built as *Razmak*) for its trans-Tasman sailings. The availability of a brand new liner at a cheap price was fortuitous indeed for Huddart Parker.

Conditional on the ship performing satisfactorily during new sea trials, Huddart Parker purchased the *Achimota* on 27th October 1932. She was renamed *Wanganella* after a small farming town in the Riverina district of New South Wales. Huddart Parker had a tradition of not using the same name twice and initially the company toyed with *Campaspe* for its new purchase. At the behest of her new owner Harland and Wolff made a number of changes to the ship, and these took six weeks to complete. The radio room was relocated to allow a nest of first class cabins on the Boat Deck, while cabins for 60 additional second class passengers were built into space originally designated for West African unberthed passengers. She could now accommodate 304 first class in 81 single-berth and 73 three-berth cabins plus two deluxe suites. Second class passengers numbered 104 in 28 two-berth and 16 three-berth cabins. A children's playroom was added and the crew accommodation was upgraded to comply with Australian maritime requirements. The front of the bridge was enclosed, doing away with Elder Dempster's characteristic bridge layout where the deck area immediately forward of the wheelhouse had been open to the weather.

Other modifications at Belfast included livestock stalls for either 38 horses or 370 sheep in the number two 'tween decks hold, while the number three 'tween decks hold was provided with 5,818 cubic feet of refrigerated space. Changes were also made to the ship's ventilation system which had been designed for West African temperatures but would now need to make the ship habitable in the much colder and windier southern ocean.

The décor of the public rooms followed the conservative fashion of the time, which can best be

The *Wanganella* at the very beginning of her long and eminent life in peace and war. In this photo she is at Belfast, having just been converted to Huddart Parker's requirements, and she is probably leaving for or returning from sea trials. Soon she will set out on the long delivery voyage to Australia. Compare the layout of deckhouses at her stern with photos of the *Wanganella* taken 25 years later. *[J. and M. Clarkson collection]*

described as opulent-country-house-goes-to-sea with a heavy emphasis on Italian and Spanish themes; the effect probably looked more appropriate in the Tasman Sea than the Bight of Benin. Huddart Parker seems to have been satisfied with the décor and furnishings chosen by Elder Dempster and changed little of it. Notable in this respect was a substantial wall mural in the first class dining room that depicted scenes from West Africa. Curiously, Huddart Parker never replaced this mural with artwork of an Australian theme. To the very end of her days the *Wanganella* retained an Elder Dempster feel about her.

The Australians took delivery of their new liner at Belfast on 27th November 1932. Two months earlier Huddart Parker had paid £345,376 to the greatly relieved management of Harland and Wolff. Costs for final work and purchases brought the total figure up to £425,000. One statistic well serves to illustrate how dire the world's economic situation was at the time: on 1st January 1931 there were 665 British merchant ships laid up totalling 2,549,200 gross tons. The worldwide recession hit the economies of Australia and New Zealand particularly hard for they were left with virtually no export markets for their foodstuffs, wool, grain and minerals. Any investment had to be made with extreme caution, even an obvious bargain such as the *Achimota*.

Trans-Tasman

The *Wanganella* finally left the yard of her birth, never to return, on 29th November 1932 under the command of Captain G.B. Bates, formerly Master of Huddart Parker's *Westralia*. Her Chief Officer was T. Laidlaw and J. Wylie was Chief Engineer. She proceeded via Gibraltar, transiting the Suez Canal and refuelling at Aden, before arrival in Sydney on 31st December where the liner was photographed passing under the newly completed Sydney Harbour Bridge. The 31-day trip from Belfast to Sydney set a record, the *Wanganella* enjoying favourable weather for the entire passage. Her maiden trans-Tasman voyage to Wellington, New Zealand began on 12th January 1933. To show off its new ship, Huddart Parker added a scenic cruise to this first voyage which took her to Fiordland in the South Island of New Zealand. After berthing in Wellington at 2.10 am on 16th January, she left Wellington for Milford Sound at 4 pm the same day with some 300 passengers, mostly Australian. The *Wanganella* returned to Wellington on 20th January and sailed immediately for Sydney. Fares for the cruise were £8 first class and £6 second.

The *Wanganella* replaced Huddart Parker's 25-year-old *Ulimaroa*, which had been withdrawn on 5th

April 1932 at the conclusion of her last voyage from New Zealand. The *Zealandia* (6,683/1910) was used temporarily until the new liner's arrival the following year. Although some contemporary publicity shows the *Wanganella* using Melbourne, her port of registry, as a terminal port, this seems to have seldom happened and the service was alternately Wellington or Auckland on one side of the Tasman and Sydney on the other. The trans-Tasman service, informally operated in tandem with the Union Steam Ship Company, offered weekly sailings in either direction. With a 14-knot service speed, this gave a three-day turn-around in the terminal ports during which plentiful general cargoes could be handled by all-too-militant antipodean stevedores. Cruises to islands of the South Pacific were made during the slack season in the mid-year southern winter. The *Wanganella* also made summer cruise voyages to the Bay of Islands in New Zealand, to Milford Sound, to Lord Howe Island in the Tasman Sea and to Hobart, Tasmania.

It did not take long for the *Wanganella* to become a well-liked and well-patronised liner. Her

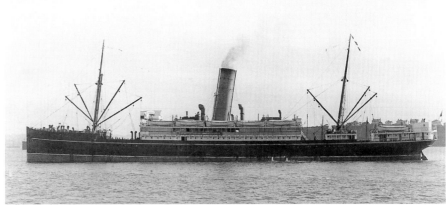

The fine-looking *Ulimaroa* – the name is an old Maori word for Australia. This was the ship the *Wanganella* replaced on Huddart Parker's trans-Tasman service in 1933. Completed at Dundee in Scotland in 1908, the 5,777 gross register tonnage *Ulimaroa* spent her entire career, with the exception of First World War service as a troopship, operating between Australia and New Zealand. As built, the *Ulimaroa* could accommodate 292 first class passengers and 121 in second. She was the biggest liner on the Tasman service for the first four years of her career. On 5th April 1932 she arrived at Sydney at the end of her last crossing from New Zealand, and between periods of lay-up was briefly employed on Huddart Parker's Sydney-Hobart route. The *Ulimaroa* was sold for demolition in Japan in 1934. *[V.H. Young and L.A. Sawyer]*

open-sided promenade decks, intended for the tropics, were not well suited to the rigours of the Tasman Sea and one complaint about her was that there was insufficient protection on her upper decks from the wind. Although Huddart Parker and the Union Steam Ship Company now had new liners on the trans-Tasman service, both remained worried by the impending threat of Matson Line's two new buildings.

Brand new, the *Wanganella* in Wellington harbour on her very first visit, late afternoon on 16th January 1933. Resuming her maiden trans-Tasman voyage, she is seen here departing for a short four day cruise to Milford Sound in the South Island of New Zealand.

The photo shows the liner as she was completed for Huddart Parker. Note the tall, dark-painted ventilators located at the forward end of her superstructure; these were later removed. The second class promenade, below the ship's mainmast, is open to the weather

and was later enclosed with windows. Behind the *Wanganella* is Mount Victoria while the large building visible between her foremast and bridge is St Gerard's Monastery. *[Alexander Turnbull Library, Wellington, New Zealand. E.T. Robson Collection, C17726]*

Above left: The *Wanganella* in Milford Sound, Fiordland, New Zealand, most probably during the cruise she made there in January 1933 during her maiden commercial voyage. Mitre Peak towers into the clouds behind her. Note that at this very early stage in her career, the *Wanganella* has open rails extending the full length of her forecastle. She would later be fitted with a solid bulwark

from her bow to about halfway along the forecastle to improve sea keeping. *[Alexander Turnbull Library, Wellington New Zealand. W. Hall Raine Collection, F20839¼]*

Above right: The Tasman crossing. The *Wanganella*, brand new and pride of the Huddart Parker fleet, going slowly astern from her berth in Wellington Harbour. Passengers bound for Sydney line her

decks and well-wishers crowd the wharf. This photo is dated 12th May 1933, four months after the liner's maiden commercial voyage. Note how the tall, unsightly ventilators mounted against her bridge front have now been painted white and are much less conspicuous. *[Alexander Turnbull Library, Wellington New Zealand. Dominion Post Collection, EP-Transport-Ships-Wanganella-01]*

Above: N.S. Falla CMG, DSO, VD. Norris Stephen Falla was born in Westport, New Zealand on 3rd May 1883 and joined the Union Steam Ship Company there as an office boy at the age of 15. By 1906 he had qualified as an accountant, and in 1909 was appointed the company's Travelling Auditor. A year later, aged 27, he became the Union Company's Assistant Traffic Manager. Norris Falla served in the New Zealand Expeditionary Force during the First World War as an artillery officer, rising to the rank of colonel. He saw action at Gallipoli and on the Western Front in France, where he was Officer Commanding the Second and Third Brigades of the New Zealand Field Artillery. Appointed

General Traffic Manager by the Union Company in 1919, then Managing Director in 1934, he became their Chairman and Managing Director in 1936. In 1940 Brigadier Falla, as he was by then, was seconded to the British Ministry of War Transport in London as New Zealand's representative. He died suddenly of a brain haemorrhage on 6th November 1945 aboard the *Port Phillip* (12,439/1942), while returning to New Zealand. Above right: Exactly where and when this photo was taken are not known,

but it is probably Wellington on a sailing day in the 1930s. The photographer is standing at the outer end of the wharf as the *Wanganella* goes slow astern past him. The rails along the *Wanganella's* promenade decks seem not particularly crowded; the same cannot be said for the profusion of cowl vents, water tanks and fan casings that surround the liner's funnels, especially her second funnel. *[Alexander Turnbull Library, Wellington, New Zealand. Dominion Post Collection, EP-Ships-Wanganella-03]*

The American pair, *Mariposa* (18,017/1931) and *Monterey* (18,017/1932), were much larger and faster, hugely subsidized by the United States Government. They were free to carry passengers on the final sector of their trans-Pacific service between Auckland and Sydney, in direct competition to the *Wanganella* and *Monowai*.

The Matson threat had long concentrated the minds of the Union Company's head office in Wellington, New Zealand and the visit in February 1934 of P&O's Chairman, Alexander Shaw, coincided with the *Monowai* making a £20,000 loss over the previous six months. In unexpected circumstances, Norris Stephen Falla (1883-1945) succeeded as Managing Director of the Union Company. The late Bill Laxon records Falla's exceptional talents as equalling those of Sir James Mills (1848-1936), the Union Company's founder. Falla saw that what was really needed was a ship capable of making the Tasman crossing in two and a half days instead of the *Monowai* and *Wanganella's* three and a half. This would require a massive increase in speed, from 14 knots to 22 knots. The order for a new ship was placed with Vickers-Armstrongs, Barrow-in-Furness on Christmas Eve 1934 and she was delivered on 28th July 1936. For £700,000 the Union Company gained the most superlative and best remembered liner ever to work the Tasman Sea. Named *Awatea* she was not, at 13,482 gross register tonnage, a large ship but her geared steam turbines were capable of up to 26 knots, making her the third fastest ship in the British Merchant Navy. For the remainder of the 1930s the *Awatea* and her legendary master Captain A.H. Davey (1878-1966) stole the show, eclipsing both the *Wanganella* and the two Matson pretenders.

The rhythm of the *Wanganella's* Tasman sailings was punctuated by a number of minor incidents during the 1930s. She had to be dry-docked for repairs after an incident on 19th September 1933 when she damaged her rudder and stern post off Berry's Bay in Sydney Harbour. On Thursday 24th June 1937 the *Wanganella* reached Auckland over 30 hours late after probably her roughest Tasman crossing during the pre-war years. The ship had been forced to heave-to for 40 hours with water up to twelve inches deep entering the crew's quarters in the fore part of the ship. Later that year, at 4.30 on the morning of 28th December 1937, she collided with the trawler *Durraween* off the coast of New South Wales,18 miles from Montague Island, while on passage between Sydney and Melbourne. There were no casualties, the *Wanganella* having 109 passengers aboard. She returned immediately to Sydney where the damage was found to be confined to shallow dents in nine waterline plates, along with minor flooding. With the liner fully booked because of the Christmas holidays, she quickly resumed service after temporary repairs. Subsequently a marine court of inquiry found the *Durraween's* master to blame for having altered course just prior to the collision, without maintaining a proper lookout.

During the second half of the 1930s the *Awatea* (1936/13,482) was to the Tasman Sea what the *Queen Mary* was to the Atlantic: the absolute best of luxury, high-speed celebrity travel. This view shows the *Awatea* in the Mersey when new and before the liner's funnels were raised during her 1937 refit at Sydney. *[B. and A. Feilden/J. and M. Clarkson collection]*

The *Wanganella* moving up Sydney Harbour on 28th December 1937, the day of her early-morning collision with the fishing boat *Durraween*. [Ian J. Farquhar collection]

Hospital ship

In late 1939 and early 1940 the war in Europe must have seemed a long way away. Except for a degree of Government control on who travelled where and when, the inter-dominion liner services continued much as they were in peacetime. Full lifeboat drills were held after departure and before reaching the open sea, and such was the threat from German commerce raiders that ships sailed blacked out at night for these were the days before radar. Then in the early hours of 19th June 1940, the war at sea suddenly became real to New Zealanders when the liner *Niagara* (13,415/1913) hit a moored mine laid by the German raider *Orion* five days previously. She was in the approaches to Auckland from where she had just sailed for Suva. Along with the *Aorangi* (17,491/1924) the *Niagara* was owned by the Canadian Australasian Line. Formed as a joint venture between the Union Steam Ship Company and the Canadian Pacific Railway Company, the Canadian Australasian Line served the long-established All Red Route between the terminal ports of Sydney and Vancouver. Inbound for Auckland at the conclusion of a routine Tasman crossing, the *Wanganella* was nearby but, because of the danger of other mines, two of which Royal New Zealand Navy sweepers duly found, she stood off from the area of the sinking. Eventually the *Wanganella* helped collect survivors from some of the *Niagara's* eighteen lifeboats, landing them safely at Auckland.

A year later the war also caught up with the *Wanganella*. Both New Zealand and Australia had large expeditionary forces deployed in North Africa and the Middle East, and it was a necessary component to this that both countries had hospital ships. The Adelaide Steamship Company's *Manunda* (9,155/1929) was the first local vessel to be taken up from trade, being requisitioned in July 1940. The *Wanganella* followed ten months later. She was requisitioned on 19th May 1941 and converted for the task ahead at Melbourne, all unnecessary fittings and furniture being landed into storage. A comprehensive range of medical facilities was installed aboard the ship. The first class lounge became the main operating theatre and passenger cabin bulkheads were stripped out for hospital wards. The largest technical modification to the *Wanganella* was to her ventilation system for the operating theatres, which meant increasing the electrical generating capacity. A new steam laundry together with an additional boiler were also fitted.

On 21st July 1941 she was commissioned at Melbourne as AHS (Australian Hospital Ship) *Wanganella*, Hospital Ship Number 45. Painted white, her hull featured a wide green band with red crosses. The ship had beds for 434 patients (increased to 548 beds by late 1943) a medical staff of 102 all of whom were from the Royal Australian Army Medical Corps, and 123 crew members. Captain Robert Darroch who in December 1938 had succeeded Captain G.B. Bates, the *Wanganella's* first master, remained in command.

At the time of her loss the *Niagara* was carrying 295 timber boxes in her strong room on D Deck, each box containing two gold ingots, all of it belonging to the Bank of England. Most of the eight tons of bullion was recovered, but the tantalising prospect of five gold ingots still somewhere inside the wreck means that the *Niagara* has not been forgotten. In recent years it has been fuel oil leaking from the wreck that has brought the *Niagara* back to the public's attention. She lies in 133 metres of water between Bream Head and Moko Hinau Island in northern New Zealand, her hull extensively broken open by gold recovery work over the decades since 19th June 1940. At the time of her loss the *Niagara* was 27 years old and had spent all her life on her owner's trans-Pacific service between Sydney and Vancouver with calls at Auckland and Honolulu. *[V.H. Young and L.A. Sawyer]*

Three photos recalling the *Wanganella's* service to Australia and New Zealand as a hospital ship during the Second World War. The above photo shows her at Brisbane. *[V.H. Young and L.A. Sawyer]*
The *Wanganella* at Singapore on 17th October 1941 (far left) where she landed an Australian Army general hospital unit. One of the hospital personnel (left) whose name, confirmed by the stencilling on his kit bag, is Smith, gives a 'thumbs up' as he disembarks. 'Digger' Smith's cheerful optimism and that of his mates will wane severely over the coming weeks as, faced with the unstoppable Japanese advance, the British and Australian army commanders on the Malayan Peninsula go from one blunder to the next. *[Imperial War Museum FE47 and FE45]*

The Commanding Officer of the *Wanganella's* medical staff was Lieutenant-Colonel F. Brown-Craig. He was the first of only three commanding officers appointed to the *Wanganella* during the whole of her war service. The other two were Lieutenant-Colonel R.L. Keniham, followed by Lieutenant-Colonel W. Freeborn. All were medical professionals who went on to distinguished careers after the war. In command of the female nursing staff aboard the *Wanganella* was the Matron; these were, successively, Mesdames Brown, Mullane, McMahon and Shaw. As with any ship, the personnel under these officers comprised many characters. Perhaps most notable among them were two Australian artists who served as medical orderlies: Loudon Saint Hill who became a famous London-based stage art designer, and Harry Miller. Many of the medical orderlies aboard the *Wanganella* had conscientious objector status.

AHS *Wanganella's* first voyage in her new role began on 31st July 1941 when she departed Melbourne for Sydney, then to Singapore via Melbourne and Fremantle with personnel of 2/13 Australian General Hospital embarked. After arriving at Singapore on 15th September and landing the hospital unit, the *Wanganella* returned to Sydney with her very first consignment of patients; 142 Australian troops suffering from tropical diseases and other illnesses. Also embarked for return to Australia were 216 mostly civilian passengers. After two days in Singapore the ship sailed for Western Australia, calling at Fremantle on 23rd September, then going on to Melbourne before reaching Sydney on 2nd October. There would be no further voyages to Singapore by AHS *Wanganella*. The sick and wounded among the 15,000 Australian troops sent there for the defence of Malaya were soon to pass into captivity when, only a few months later, the city fell to the advancing Japanese on 15th February 1942.

The *Wanganella's* second voyage took her to Suez in Egypt to uplift wounded for repatriation home to Australia. While at Port Tewfik the hospital ship experienced her first action when the port was bombed by enemy aircraft on mistaken intelligence that the *Queen Elizabeth* (83,673/1940) was there. After two further trips to the Middle East the *Wanganella* was sent in May 1942 to Port Moresby, New Guinea, to evacuate casualties from the fighting against the Japanese at Kokoda. After returning to Sydney she went back to Port Tewfik, this time to bring wounded New Zealand army personnel home to Wellington. Crossing to Sydney, the *Wanganella* next proceeded to Townsville, from where she sailed for Melbourne with wounded American servicemen aboard.

From October 1943 until March 1944 AHS *Wanganella* was loaned to the New Zealand Government while their hospital ship *Maunganui* (7,527/1911) was under repair in England after breaking a tail shaft. During this period the *Wanganella* made three trips to evacuate invalid New Zealand personnel from Italy and Egypt. In total the *Wanganella* completed 19 voyages as a hospital ship; taking her to the Mediterranean and throughout the Pacific War theatre. She carried a total of 13,385 patients and covered 251,611 miles.

The most notable event in the *Wanganella's* war service occurred at Bombay Harbour on the afternoon of 14th April 1944, during her thirteenth voyage as a hospital ship. The *Fort Stikine* (7,142/1942) with 1,417 tons of ammunition and explosives in her lower holds, was discharging cotton bales stowed in her 'tween decks when a fire broke out among the bales in number two hold. The flames spread out of control and ignited the ammunition, causing two catastrophic blasts 34 minutes apart. The surrounding area of the Bombay docks was devastated by the explosions and subsequent fires, which killed up to 730 people and injured 3,000. Twelve merchant ships were sunk or damaged beyond repair. One hundred and twenty four bars of gold that the *Fort Stikine* was carrying were also lost. The *Wanganella* had been moored some two miles away but was moved to an inner anchorage where many of the injured were brought to the ship, her surgical staff working continuously for 36 hours. She remained in Bombay for a week before resuming her voyage to Taranto, Italy, where she embarked New Zealand wounded for Wellington and Lyttelton.

On her next voyage to Taranto, sailing via Colombo, the *Wanganella* on 16th July 1944 came upon the wreckage of the Eastern and Australian Steam Ship Company's liner *Tanda* (8,650/1914). She had been torpedoed off Mangalore, India, by a German submarine the previous night. A search was made for survivors but none were located. They had all been landed at Colombo and on her return from the Mediterranean the *Wanganella* uplifted those among them who had been injured.

An almost forgotten incident during the Second World War, in which the *Wanganella* played a small part, was the extraordinary affair of the Dutch Shell tanker *Ondina* (6,341/1939). On 11th November 1942 the *Ondina* was in ballast out of Fremantle, Western Australia, bound for Diego Garcia in the Indian Ocean when she was intercepted 550 nautical miles south-south-west of the Cocos Islands by two Japanese commerce raiders. These were the 10,438-ton *Hokoku Maru* and the 10,437-ton *Aikoku Maru*. Both were converted liners each with a speed of 21 knots and armed with eight 5.5 inch guns and four torpedo tubes. Escorting the *Ondina* was the Indian Navy's Australian-built corvette *Bengal*. While HMIS *Bengal* took on one of the raiders the *Ondina's* gun crew manned the ship's single 4-inch gun and commenced one of the most gallant actions of the war at sea. After a ranging shot at the *Hokoku Maru* 8,000 yards away, the *Ondina's* fifth shot hit the Japanese ship aft. An

Built in 1914 for British India, the 6,956 gross register tonnage *Tanda* was sold without name change in 1924 to the Eastern and Australian Steam Ship Company for use on its Australia, Japan and China service. She was operating between Australia and India, having been requisitioned for the Liner Division, when torpedoed by *U 181* on 15th July 1944. *[V.H. Young and L.A. Sawyer]*

The tanker *Ondina* in war rig. Built by Nederlandse Droogdok Mij., Amsterdam in 1939, the 12-knot *Ondina* was one of a class of seven similar modern tankers ordered by La Corona, the Dutch part of Shell, for carriage of oil products from the Dutch East Indies. She was in South East Asian waters when Germany conquered Holland, and was nearby when the Japanese invaded Java in 1942. Three of the *Ondina's* sisters became war losses. So famous was the *Ondina* that after she was sold for scrap a new vessel delivered in 1961 perpetuated her name. *[Ian J. Farquhar collection]*

A twin screw motorship, one of three sisters, *Hokoku Maru* was built for Osaka Shosen K.K. and launched on 5th July 1939. Intended for her owner's Japan to Europe service, the *Hokoko Maru* was taken over in August 1941 for conversion to an armed merchant cruiser. On 10th March 1942 she was commissioned as a warship of the Imperial Japanese Navy. Her service in this role proved as brief as her time as a passenger liner. *[John Marsh collection]*

enormous explosion followed, blowing off the *Hokoku Maru's* stern and causing her to sink. Extensively damaged and ablaze from the surviving raider's gunfire, hit by two torpedoes and with all ammunition expended, the *Ondina's* crew of 56 abandoned ship only to be machine-gunned in their lifeboats. Captain W. Horsman, the *Ondina's* Master, had been killed by a direct hit on the bridge just after giving the order to abandon ship. The *Aikoku Maru* then broke off the attack to pick up the *Hokoku Maru's* survivors.

There next followed a repeat of the salvage of another tanker, the *San Demetrio* and her famous story from 1940. The *Ondina* did not sink. Her surviving crew reboarded the tanker and, having extinguished the fires, found her hull to be largely watertight and her engines undamaged. Restarting the engines,

by nightfall they were heading back to Fremantle. Six days later the *Ondina* rendezvoused with the *Wanganella* and transferred her wounded to the hospital ship. On 18th November both ships reached Fremantle. HMIS *Bengal* also survived, arriving at Diego Garcia on 17th November.

Perhaps the most poignant of all the *Wanganella's* wartime passengers were the survivors of Japanese prisoner-of-war camps in South East Asia, who were nursed back to health on voyages home. In September 1945, immediately following the Japanese surrender, the *Wanganella* went first to the island of Morotai just south of the Philippines, then across to Labuan on the island of Borneo, and lastly to Kuching in Sarawak where she anchored on 12th September. Australian prisoners of war, newly released from local camps and dreadfully emaciated, were ferried out to the ship in small boats. Further POWs were embarked on the return journey, with the *Wanganella* berthing in Sydney on 20th October. Her very final voyage as a hospital ship began a week later, bringing home more POWs. She sailed from Labuan on 10th November and arrived back at Sydney on 23rd November, her war service at an end.

Hospital ships had lonely wars. They did not sail in convoys, they were fully lit at night, carried designated markings and their passage plans were widely advised to all, including hostile parties. There is no doubt that Harland and Wolff built quality and this, combined with Huddart Parker's high standards of maintenance and the dedication of both her crew and her medical staff, ensured that all the voyages the *Wanganella* made during her war career came to safe conclusions.

Barrett Reef

Decommissioned and returned to Huddart Parker late in 1945, the *Wanganella* was refitted in Melbourne to carry 316 first class and 108 second class passengers. The liner retained her pre-war appearance except for the deckhouse at her stern, which had a second level added for improved crew accommodation. The open sides outboard of number three hatch, part of the first class promenade, were plated over to give better protection against the weather. Sixty-nine year old Captain Robert Darroch resumed command after having been the *Wanganella's* Master throughout the war years.

With her refit completed in September 1946 the *Wanganella* was once more in her owner's livery of buff funnels and black hull. At the time there was considerable demand from intending passengers wanting to travel to North America following the end of the war, so before recommencing Huddart Parker's trans-Tasman service the *Wanganella* made a round trip across the Pacific. She departed Sydney on 31st October 1946, calling at Auckland and Honolulu before going on to Vancouver where she docked on 23rd November. Eleven days later, on 4th December, the *Wanganella* sailed from Vancouver to return to Australia. Again calling at Honolulu and Auckland, she was back at Sydney by 28th December.

At 12.25 pm on 16th January 1947 the *Wanganella* left Sydney to begin her first post-war Tasman crossing to Wellington, the occasion being marked with great fanfare. She had a full complement of passengers but, apart from mails and ship's stores, was carrying no cargo. The weather stayed fine and by the evening of Sunday 19th January the *Wanganella* was in Cook Strait between the North and South Islands of New Zealand, steering east by south for the entrance to Wellington Harbour. The Fourth Officer, T.F. Gibson, had the watch but Captain Darroch was on the bridge navigating the ship. The sea was almost flat calm with a light northerly breeze and the night clear but dark with no moon.

The *Wanganella* passed Karori Rock at 10.43 pm and shortly afterwards Pencarrow Light, marking the eastern side of the harbour entrance, was sighted on the port bow. As he stood in towards the entrance, Captain Darroch ordered easy port helm to begin lining up his ship with the front and rear leading lights. These are the two light beacons inside Wellington Harbour, one positioned approximately 1.25 miles behind the other, that mark the narrow, deep water entrance channel between the Pencarrow shore and, to the west, the wave-swept rocks of Barrett Reef.

Searching with his binoculars, Captain Darroch saw a white flashing light ahead, together with another flashing light, much dimmer, behind it. Identifying these as the two leading lights, he steered the *Wanganella* on a course for what he thought was the front, southern-most light. Captain Darroch knew that Barrett Reef was also marked by a white flashing light. Because the intervals in flashes for the lights he had observed seemed to differ from the interval given on the chart for the Barrett Reef light, the Master concluded that this light was either not visible or not operating.

His decision in this regard was entirely mistaken. The light Captain Darroch was heading for, which he believed to be the front leading light, was in reality the flashing light on a buoy marking the southern extremity of Barrett Reef. The dimmer light he had seen was the first of the leading lights and it was this for which he should have been steering. The ship continued on her course for a further ten minutes until the seaman lookout on the forecastle suddenly called 'rocks ahead!' Seconds later, at 11.35 pm, the *Wanganella* went onto Barrett Reef. Moving at 13 knots she struck Outer Rock at the reef's southern edge and came to a stop.

The impact totally crushed the *Wanganella's* forefoot and her underwater hull below number one hold, splitting and mangling plates and forcing up her tank tops. Two holes, the larger one 40 feet by 22 feet, were torn open on the port side of number two hold, the rocks penetrating the ship and impaling her on the reef. Bottom and side plating was ripped, dented and crumpled for nearly 200 feet as far aft as the fore bulkhead to the engine spaces. Both forward holds filled quickly with water to a depth of 17 feet. The Master ordered hard a starboard helm and full astern on both engines. On finding that the *Wanganella* was held fast, he then ordered the ship's Chief Engineer, J. Wylie, to keep his engines at slow ahead so that the ship stayed on the reef until all passengers could be evacuated.

The *Wanganella's* Chief Officer, W.G. Ferris, had also been on the bridge when the ship grounded, arriving there five minutes earlier. Although not on watch, he had wanted to familiarise himself with the harbour entrance, having not been into Wellington for ten years. When she struck, Ferris pulled the engine telegraphs to stop and immediately left the bridge, hurrying forward to shut the watertight doors. All lifeboats were then swung out under his direction.

Staff on duty at the Beacon Hill Signal Station, located on the hilltop above Breaker Bay overlooking Barrett Reef, heard the *Wanganella* strike after having watched her approach the harbour entrance. Assistance was quickly provided. The first ship to reach the *Wanganella* was the Canterbury Steam Shipping Company's coaster *Gale* (622/1935) which had been proceeding to sea from Wellington at the time. She stood by the *Wanganella* until tugs arrived. From Wellington the Harbour Master despatched the tugs *Toia* (423/1919) and *Terawhiti* (260/1907). In addition, the tender *Natone* (73/1900), the pilot boat *Arahina* (36/1925) and the harbour ferry *Cobar* (157/1903) were sent to take off the *Wanganella's* passengers. The first passengers began arriving at Queens Wharf in Wellington just prior to daybreak the following morning, luggage and mail being transferred ashore later on 20th January. There were no casualties among either the passengers or crew.

Daylight revealed the *Wanganella* listing slightly to starboard, the black mass of Outer Rock right under her starboard bow. Her situation could not have been more precarious. She had gone aground at high tide so that at low water the bulk of Outer Rock seemed all the more formidable. The full rock-crowded panorama of Barrett Reef lay to the north, directly in front of the ship. She was pinned at the bow, the reef rising near-vertically from the sea floor with the after two-thirds of the ship in water fifty feet deep. Immense wrenching and buckling forces were thereby exerted on her hull, the after portion rising and falling with the seas and tides while her bow was held fast. From behind, the *Wanganella* was exposed to the southerly gales and heavy seas for which Cook Strait and the harbour entrance are notorious. It was imperative that she be moved off the reef and into shelter as quickly as possible.

Non-essential crew were taken ashore, 18 remaining aboard in addition to ship's officers. Six hundred tons of fuel oil were pumped overboard to lighten the ship. The first attempt to free the *Wanganella* began at 11.15 pm on Monday 20th January, the night following her stranding, using the

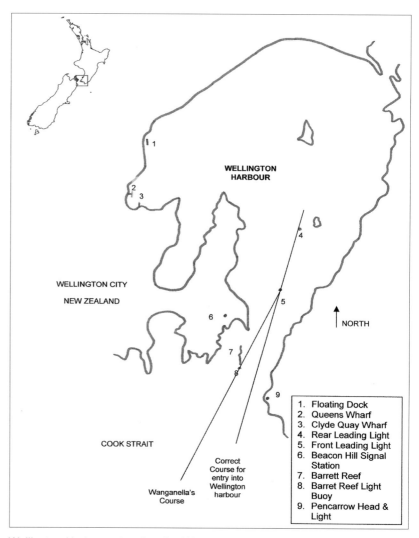

Wellington Harbour, showing the *Wanganella's* approach on the night of 19th January 1947.

1. Floating Dock
2. Queens Wharf
3. Clyde Quay Wharf
4. Rear Leading Light
5. Front Leading Light
6. Beacon Hill Signal Station
7. Barrett Reef
8. Barret Reef Light Buoy
9. Pencarrow Head & Light

Union Steam Ship Company's *Terawhiti*. Built in 1907, the *Terawhiti* was a powerful salvage tug based in Wellington. But there was to be no quick release from the reef's custody and so the tug *Kahanui* was brought south from the port of Wanganui to assist. A third tug, the Wellington Harbour Board's *Toia*, was made available on stand-by.

A second effort to move the stranded liner commenced two days later at 4 am on Wednesday 22nd January, taking advantage of a flood tide. With the *Wanganella* going full astern on her engines, all three tugs applied their combined power to towing wires while her winches hauled on cables linked to a spread of mushroom anchors placed aft of the ship.

She could not be moved. Miraculously the weather stayed fine and the southerly gales stayed away. The liner's predicament was a major news sensation, followed daily by all of New Zealand which, in 1947, had a population of 1.8 million people. Because of her role as a hospital ship bringing home casualties from the war in Italy and North Africa, the *Wanganella* was very well known. She was the fifteenth ship, and by far the largest, to have struck Barrett Reef during the history of European settlement in New Zealand. Under headlines such as 'fight for

An aerial view of the stranded liner, most probably taken the day after she went onto Barrett Reef. Outer Rock is clearly visible immediately to the left of the *Wanganella's* bow, and the Union Steam Ship Company's tender *Natone* is alongside for transfer of passengers' luggage. Disturbed water at the *Wanganella's* stern indicates her propellers are turning slowly to hold the liner in position on the reef until damage to her hull can be assessed fully. Water from the flooded number two hold is being discharged overboard just forward of the *Wanganella's* bridge. *[Ian J. Farquhar collection]*

liner' and 'grave fears held', newspapers carried what for the time were dramatic reports about explosives being used to break the reef's grip on the *Wanganella* should the tugs fail to extricate her. 'Tugs cease work' said the headlines on 28th January, nine days after the stranding, and the ship's prospects seemed even more desperate. After prolonged efforts trying to shift the *Wanganella*, the crews of all three tugs - *Toia*, *Terawhiti* and *Kahanui* - had gone on strike until they received higher wages.

Salvage efforts meanwhile were under the direction of Huddart Parker's Marine Engineering Superintendent, D.E. Eadie, who arrived by plane from Australia. Also hastening across the Tasman were Captain G. McDonald, Marine Underwriter and Surveyor for Huddart Parker, and John E. Johnstone, a Melbourne diver famous for his involvement with recovery of gold from the sunken *Niagara*. Assisting them was J. Dilworth, a consulting engineer and adviser to the London Salvage Association.

Johnstone flew into Wellington on Saturday 25th January, six days after the stranding, and next day commenced his first underwater inspection of the *Wanganella*. He described the ruptured tank top plating inside number two hold as 'working

John E. Johnstone (above right) of Melbourne, who was chief diver during salvage operations aboard the *Wanganella*. Next to him (at left) is Huddart Parker's Captain G. McDonald, also of Melbourne.

23

The engines-aft motor coaster *Gale* was heading out through the entrance to Wellington Harbour when the *Wanganella* struck, and was the first ship to go to her assistance. Built by Scott and Sons of Bowling on the Clyde, who launched her in August 1935, she served the coastal ports of New Zealand for her owners the Canterbury Steam Shipping Company until December 1962 when sold to Asian buyers. *[Ian J. Farquhar collection]*

The salvage tug *Terawhiti* (above left) owned by the Union Steam Ship Company, played a major role in the successful removal of the *Wanganella* from Barrett Reef. Forty years old at the time of the stranding, the *Terawhiti* was sold later in 1947 to Australian owners.

In this photo she is alongside the Union Company's *Rangatira* (6,152/1931) after a mishap in 1936. The pilot launch *Arahina* (above right) owned and operated by the Wellington Harbour Board, as she was in February 1947 when sent to Barrett Reef to take passengers off the *Wanganella*.

Built in Auckland in 1925, her wheelhouse and funnel were much altered during a two year refit that began in 1954. The *Arahina* also played a key role in the next mishap involving Barrett Reef, the much more serious *Wahine* disaster of 10th April 1968. *[Both: V.H. Young and L.A. Sawyer]*

The harbour ferry *Cobar* (left) which, like the *Arahina*, took passengers ashore from the stranded *Wanganella*. In 1947 she did not look quite as pretty as she does in this photo; by then both masts had been removed and her lower passenger deck had been enclosed. Built at Sydney in 1906 for the Cobar Copper Mining Company, the *Cobar* was purchased by Wellington Harbour Ferries Ltd. in April 1906 for use on their service to Days Bay and Eastbourne. A 96-ton wooden-hulled steamer, for over 40 years she was a very familiar sight on Wellington Harbour. In March 1948 she caught fire while berthed at Days Bay Wharf. Although repaired, she failed a Marine Department survey and ended up in the Chatham Islands (east of New Zealand) as a fish freezer barge. Her loss came as the result of another fire, this one on 6th March 1958. *[Ian J. Farquhar collection]*

Passengers from the *Wanganella* arriving at Queens Wharf in Wellington aboard the Wellington Harbour Board's pilot boat *Arahina* (right), early on the morning of Monday 20th January 1947. Among the *Wanganella's* passengers was Admiral of the Fleet Sir John Tovey RN. His presence must have added considerably to Captain Darroch's embarrassment, for Tovey had commanded the British naval force that sank the German battleship *Bismarck* less than six years earlier in May 1941. The admiral and his wife were on a private visit to New Zealand. Also travelling aboard the *Wanganella* was the British car manufacturer Lord Nuffield. *[Ian J. Farquhar collection]*

A panoramic view looking west towards the rocks and hills of Palmer Head in the middle distance behind the *Wanganella* (below). The area of water between Palmer Head and the liner is Chaffers Passage. In the far distance, houses snake along the beach front and ridge lines of Lyall Bay. This photo was most likely taken the day after the stranding. *[Ian J. Farquhar collection]*

The Wellington Harbour Board's tug *Toia* (Captain J. E. Hancox) standing by the *Wanganella* with towing wires made fast to the liner's stern, 6th February 1947. *Toia* is waiting for any indication the *Wanganella* may at last free herself from the reef as high tide and the compressors driving air into the forward holds take their effect. Behind the two ships are the Pencarrow Hills on the eastern side of Wellington Harbour. The original of this photo has a hand-written entry concerning the yacht at right: 'Keeler yacht *Ilex*, recently back from Sydney, lends a hand in the salvage operations. The small craft's wireless was used for communication between the tugs and the shore.' Exactly why the *Toia's* radio equipment was unable to link her with the shore is not clear; perhaps the yacht's role was to monitor radio traffic in the event of some sudden development in the *Wanganella's* incarceration on the reef. *([an J. Farquhar collection]*

Seamen peer over the side of the *Wanganella's* forecastle as low water exposes the damage to the liner's bow as well as the full above-water mass of Outer Rock (above). The Wellington Harbour ferry *Cobar* is in the distance at left, the tug *Toia* at right. *[Ian J. Farquhar collection]*

The stricken liner photographed on 7th February 1947, listing slightly, her bow now much deeper in the water, her port accident boat partially lowered and with Outer Rock looking very menacing right beside the *Wanganella's* bow. *[Ian J. Farquhar collection]*

The *Wanganella* photographed from the bridge of a small vessel coming alongside, possibly the day after the stranding. Outer Rock is again clearly visible. *[Museum of Wellington, City and Sea, New Zealand. Neg No. 6016]*

like gigantic scissors', screeching and bending with the constant movement of the ship. The sea surged relentlessly in and out of the huge 40 by 22 feet gash in the side of the hold, making diving work the most hazardous he had ever encountered. From his survey of the *Wanganella's* hull Johnstone found the ship to be grounded on three ledges of rock and straining badly with the ebb and flow of the tides. In addition to the two forward holds, the stores hold directly aft of number two hold had been pierced by the reef just fifteen inches in front of the engine room bulkhead.

The solution was to make the forward part of the *Wanganella's* hull sufficiently buoyant so that during a full flood tide it would lift clear of the highest rock pinnacles holding the liner. She could then be towed off the reef. The task as such was relatively straightforward but it could only be accomplished if the weather stayed calm. The chances of this were felt to be negligible. Every day of good weather was precious and so work now began at maximum speed to lighten the ship by sealing her two forward holds and blowing compressed air into them. Additional pumps were taken out to the *Wanganella* to relieve pressure on the vital bulkheads between the number two hold, the stores hold and the ship's engine spaces. If a bulkhead collapsed, the *Wanganella* would probably have broken her back. Some 35 'shore labourers', as they were described, were put to work inside the flooded holds, removing steel armour plate and concrete slabs that formed the ship's ballast.

Numerous air compressors were delivered to the liner, hoisted aboard from the tugs using the *Wanganella's* derricks. The two forward hatches were sealed by welding steel plates over them, then compressed air was driven into the holds to force the sea out. Diving and salvage work aboard and alongside the grounded liner was tense and hazardous, a fact probably not well appreciated by the hundreds of sightseers and picnickers who came to view the *Wanganella* from nearby headlands and beaches each day. The terrific roar from the many compressors was plainly audible on shore. On 2nd February the only fatality of the stranding occurred. A 61-year-old greaser from Sydney was evacuated from the ship on the evening of 24 January aboard the pilot launch *Arahina*, after falling and fracturing his skull while on duty in the *Wanganella's* engine room. He died in Wellington Hospital eight days later.

By Friday 31st January work in the forward holds was sufficiently advanced for another big attempt at pulling the *Wanganella* clear of the reef. But this also met with disappointment and so renewed efforts were made to ensure the hatches and all ventilator openings were completely sealed. Tension mounted as the holds were pressurized further and winches hauled on the tackle laid to the mushroom anchors astern of her. Finally, on the afternoon of Thursday

6th February, the eighteenth day she had been aground, the men aboard the *Wanganella* felt her start to move. Word spread rapidly across Wellington city: 'the *Wanganella's* coming off the reef!'. Hundreds of cars began converging on shoreline roads and vantage points opposite the ship. At around 9 pm that night, rising and falling to a southerly swell, the *Wanganella* was seen to be swinging to starboard. Her stern came round to the south-east, pointing across the harbour entrance to line up with Pencarrow Head.

It was a warm summer's evening and the liner was lit up brilliantly. Car horns blared and cheering could be heard across the water as, at 9.10 pm, the *Wanganella* was pulled clear of the reef by the tug *Toia*, which had a line onto the ship's stern. Also at the stern, sparks flew in showers as the cables holding her to the mushroom anchors were hurriedly cut away. Loud grinding and tearing sounds told of further mutilation to the ship's hull as she was dragged from the rocks that had held her. Stern-first, heavily down by the bow and watched by thousands of people, the *Wanganella* was towed very slowly up the harbour by the *Toia*, with the *Terawhiti* steadying her bow and the *Kahanui* standing by. The *Wanganella* was placed alongside Aotea Quay by 11.30 pm, her bow drawing 39 feet 6 inches and resting on the harbour bottom. Sightseers crowded the wharf beside the ship long into the night.

Repairs

For days afterwards newspapers throughout New Zealand and Australia carried the astonishing story of the *Wanganella*. Foremost in the drama of her escape was the amazingly calm, settled weather throughout the period while she was on Barrett Reef. Storm-force winds and seas are commonplace in Cook Strait and around the entrance to Wellington Harbour. Had a 'southerly blow' occurred during the 18 days the *Wanganella* was aground, she would very likely have become a total wreck. Two or three southerly weather fronts had approached the Cook Strait area but remarkably they had all weakened and died away. Equal contributor to her liberation was the strength and skill of the *Wanganella's* construction by Harland and Wolff. This had enabled the ship to withstand the enormous stress her hull and bulkheads had been placed under.

Freeing her from Barrett Reef was a major salvage achievement but it would be December 1948 before the liner was restored to her owner's service. Pumps and air compressors reduced her draft by the bow to 24 feet 11 inches but the *Wanganella* had to wait until Wellington's Jubilee Floating Dock was vacated by another ship before she was moved there, under her own power, on the afternoon of 18th February 1947. Captain Darroch and Captain D.M. Todd, the Deputy Harbour Master, succeeded in

Right: Friday 7th February 1947, the day after the *Wanganella* was freed from Barrett Reef. With pumps and compressors temporarily shut down, her bow, its underwater destruction yet to be revealed, has been allowed to settle into the mud beside Aotea Quay. Alongside the liner is the tug *Karaka* (43/1911). The Jubilee Floating Dock, located close-by, was occupied by another ship and the *Wanganella* had to wait eleven days until she could be moved there and lifted out of the water. *[Alexander Turnbull Library, Wellington New Zealand. EP-Transport-Ships-Wanganella-02]*

The *Wanganella* is the largest but not the last ship to have had her bottom torn open by the rocks of Barrett Reef. Just over 21 years later, in a much more disastrous incident, the Union Steam Ship Company's *Wahine* (8,944/1966) went onto the reef in extremely heavy weather, while entering Wellington Harbour early on the morning of 10th April 1968. A total of 734 passengers and crew were aboard. The *Wahine* came off the rocks but sank later that day, after an epic battle on the part of her Master, Captain H.G. Robertson, his crew and the tug *Tapuhi* to save her. Fifty one people lost their lives.

Below: The pumps and compressors have been restarted and the *Wanganella* is precariously afloat again, leaning towards the wharf. Her engines are standing-by and she is about to be moved onto the floating dock. Note her starboard anchor has been removed. All seems quiet aboard and around the *Wanganella* but, below decks on the liner and on the tugs attending her, another round of strikes for more wages is being cooked up. The *Wanganella* was a hotbed of industrial troubles from the very beginning of her long ordeal in Wellington, with every union that had workers involved with her seeking more money. *[Alexander Turnbull Library, Wellington New Zealand. New Zealand Free Lance Collection, PAColl – 8602-32]*

With no tugs to assist - they are nearby but with their seamen on strike - the *Wanganella* is manoeuvred very carefully under her own engine power into the floating dock on 18th February 1947 (above), where she will be finally out of danger. *[Ian J. Farquhar collection]*

The *Wanganella* almost inside the floating dock. Captain David Todd, Wellington Deputy Harbour Master, can be seen on the port wing of the *Wanganella's* bridge; he is standing at the top of the steps that gave access to the vertical ladder on the forward face of the liner's superstructure. This would not be the last occasion on which the extraordinary ship handling skills of Captain Todd would be called upon for vessels damaged and disabled in Wellington Harbour. Three years later he performed an even more remarkable feat in getting the cargo liner *Taranaki* (11,300/1928) back into port with the coaster *Waipiata* (2,826/1926) wedged at right angles across her bow, after a night-time collision. *[Ian J. Farquhar collection]*

placing the *Wanganella* on the dock without the aid of tugs or seamen, all of whom had gone on strike for bonus payments two hours earlier. The ship was in more danger while being transferred onto the dock than she had been the whole time on Barrett Reef. Only the labouring air compressors were keeping her afloat. Had part of the deck around the forward hatches given way under the air pressure beneath, the resulting explosion would have been like the ship hitting a mine. But good fortune again served the *Wanganella*. Once out of the water and with the compressors at last switched off, the extensive damage to the fore part of the ship's hull was fully revealed. It was much worse than Huddart Parker and the salvage men had expected, due in large part to additional twisting and tearing of plates and frames when the ship swung free from the reef's grip. Most dramatically of all, the *Wanganella's* port anchor could be seen embedded in the wreckage of stem plates ripped and folded back upon each other by their impact with the reef.

The striking seamen were awarded a bonus of 15 shillings an hour above their normal wages, but the dock workers also wanted more money before they would start clearing the mud and debris from the forward holds. There were also large quantities of rotting food to be shovelled out of the *Wanganella's* stores hold. The *Wanganella* was declared 'black' until the wage demands were met. She sat in the dock for three months, costing Huddart Parker £8,000 in dock fees. Her bow temporarily patched with concrete and with pumps and compressors again working non-stop, the *Wanganella* was refloated on 27th May and towed across the inner harbour to Clyde Quay Wharf. There she was laid up awaiting permanent repairs, kept afloat by compressed air for the next eight months.

Just before she entered the floating dock the *Wanganella's* crew were paid off and repatriated to Australia aboard the Union Steam Ship Company's elderly *Wahine* (4,436/1913). A small number of

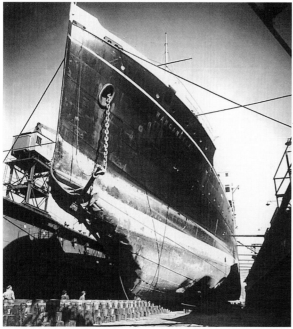

Above left: Destruction to the forefoot of the *Wanganella*, viewed from the floor of the Jubilee Floating Dock in Wellington. Huddart Parker had not anticipated that the *Wanganella's* bow would be so totally destroyed, but to New Zealanders familiar with Wellington's climate it seemed nothing short of a miracle that the ship had survived at all. Cook Strait and the entrance to Wellington Harbour are, warns the New Zealand Pilot, subject to 'the worst storms experienced in New Zealand waters.' Yet for eighteen days while the *Wanganella* lay captive on Barrett Reef, conditions stayed fine and tranquil. So remarkable was this that the term 'Wanganella Weather'"entered the New Zealand language: an extraordinarily long spell of sunny skies, light airs and mild temperatures uninterrupted by the usual battering from high seas and freezing winds. *[Alexander Turnbull Library, Wellington New Zealand. W Hall Raine Collection, G18032 1/1]*

Above right: Workers peer out through one of the gashes in the side of number two hold after the *Wanganella* was raised out of the sea in the floating dock. The damage to the liner's forward hull was too severe and too widespread for her plates and frames to be repaired; an entire new section of hull some 200 feet long from bow to engine room was needed, and would have to come from Belfast on the other side of the world. *[Ian J. Farquhar Collection]*

Below: A fine shot of the *Wanganella* going slow astern out of the Wellington floating dock under her own power on 27th May 1947. She has been in the dock for 14 weeks following her sojourn on Barrett Reef, and concrete has been used to make her bow as watertight as possible. For the first time since her stranding, the *Wanganella* is afloat on an even keel. An eight month wait now lies ahead for the ship. She will be laid up at Clyde Quay in Wellington until the steel for permanent repairs is delivered from Harland and Wolff in Belfast. Note the *Wanganella's* empty lifeboat davits and that her anchors have also been unshipped. *[Alexander Turnbull Library, Wellington, New Zealand. EP-Ships-Wanganella-02]*

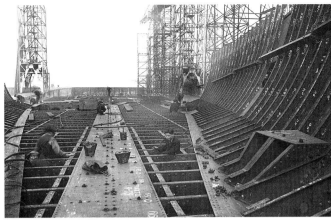

After filing them away when they had built her as the *Achimota* nearly two decades earlier, Harland and Wolff retrieved their plans for the hull of the *Wanganella* and laid down a new bow section on one of their vacant slipways at Queen's Island, Belfast. These three photos show work well advanced. *[Ulster Folk and Transport Museum, 10682, 10691 and 10692]*

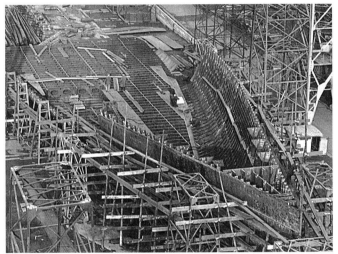

seamen and motormen needed to work the ship remained aboard. With no other liner available, the *Wahine* was placed on the trans-Tasman run as a temporary replacement for the *Wanganella*. Built for the Union Company's overnight service between Wellington and Lyttelton, the *Wahine* had limited facilities for passengers and so numbers had to be restricted to 300. She departed Wellington on 11th February 1947 for the first of 26 return crossings she made during 1947 and 1948.

The contract for erection of new, replacement steel for the *Wanganella's* forward hull was awarded to the local firm of William Cable and Co. Ltd. Harland and Wolff supplied a complete new double bottom that was nearly 200 feet long from the stem to the engine room bulkhead, and 16 feet in height from the keel to the ship's waterline. It was constructed on one of Harland and Wolff's slipways at Belfast in the same manner as with a new ship, the keel being laid and the double bottom and tank top being assembled and plated. Main framing was then erected together with the shell plating and the lower deck beams and girders. A new forepeak bulkhead was prefabricated and erected with all riveting complete. As much riveting as possible was done,

then the entire structure was dismantled with each piece being carefully marked. Next it was shipped by coaster from Belfast to Liverpool for loading aboard the New Zealand Shipping Company's *Hororata* (13,945/1942).

Meanwhile in Wellington the *Wanganella* was placed back in the floating dock on 20th January 1948. The damaged bow and underwater hull were cut away and the forepart of the ship shored and braced. When the *Hororata* berthed at Wellington in early March work commenced on assembling the new bow. It was done under the direction of L. Hamilton, Assistant Works Manager from Harland and Wolff, who had travelled to New Zealand along with two foremen from the shipyard. The work was completed on 28th October after 283 days in the floating dock, some 100 new plates and a total of 400 tons of steel being required. The following morning, 29th October 1948, the dock was lowered gradually until the *Wanganella* was sitting at a draught of eleven feet. Flotation tests were then carried out, the new plating being searched for leaks. Only one minor leak was found, the dock being raised by two feet until it was plugged. After lunch and in a strengthening north-westerly breeze, the dock was lowered fully until the *Wanganella* was afloat. She was towed out of the

The *Wanganella* undergoing repairs in Wellington's Jubilee Floating Dock. The photo shows a timber barrier erected on the floor of the dock at its landward end to shelter workers from the wintry north-westerly winds. Presumably it was also there to shield the massive damage to the *Wanganella's* bow from the gaze of commuters entering and leaving Wellington City each day on nearby roads and train lines. The *Wanganella's* resumption of trans-Tasman sailings following the end of the Second World War had been widely anticipated; no doubt the managers of Huddart Parker wished to spare themselves any further bad publicity after the ship's maiden post-war voyage to New Zealand had ended in such embarrassment.

The Jubilee Floating Dock was so named to mark the 50th anniversary in 1931 of the founding of the Wellington Harbour Board. The dock had a lifting capacity of 17,000 tons and was built at Wallsend-on-Tyne, England, in 1931 by Swan, Hunter and Wigham Richardson Ltd., then towed out to New Zealand by the Dutch tugs *Witte Zee* and *Zwarte Zee*. It arrived in Wellington Harbour on 29th December 1931. On 28th December 1988, 57 years later almost to the day, the dock was towed from Wellington bound for Bangkok and new owners. Five days into the voyage it broke in two during heavy weather while in the middle of the Tasman Sea. The dock's fore section sank immediately, the remainder of the dock went to the bottom six days afterwards. *[V.H. Young and L.A. Sawyer]*

Rebuilding the *Wanganella's* forefoot and lower forward hull after the damaged sections had been cut away and new prefabricated steel had arrived from Harland and Wolff in Belfast. The repairs to the *Wanganella* were plagued by industrial trouble and in this photo work appears to be proceeding at a leisurely pace. Only a few workers are visible, erection of replacement framing is not yet completed while the casting for the new stem can be seen lying on the floor of the dock at lower left, beneath the trestles. Just to the right of this, also on the dock floor, part of a brazier for heating rivets can be made out, along with the head and shoulders of the worker operating it. White hot rivets will be thrown up to the hatted man kneeling on the tank top, pneumatic rivet gun in hand. This photo is dated April 1948. *[Alexander Turnbull Library, Wellington New Zealand. New Zealand Free Lance Collection, PAColl – 8602-31]*

The new steel for her bow fully in place and freshly painted, the *Wanganella* is floated out of the submerged Jubilee Floating Dock (at left) on 29th October 1948, after 17 months there. Wellington has acquired two new tugs during this interval, both owned by the Union Steam Ship Company. At left is the *Taioma* (232/1944) while her near-sister *Tapuhi* (232/1945) is at right. At far right, her starboard side to the camera, is the veteran tug *Toia* (423/1919). Taken to Auckland in May 1949, she was laid up there and scrapped from 1955. The area of water in the foreground, at right of the dock mooring wharf, is now occupied by the Cook Strait 'Interislander' rail ferry terminal. [*Ian J. Farquhar collection*]

Captain H. F. Norrie, appointed by Huddart Parker to take command of the *Wanganella* just before her repairs were finished, photographed on the liner's bridge during her sea trials in Cook Strait (right). These were held on 29th and 30th November 1948. Captain Norrie was the *Wanganella's* permanent master for the next ten years until he retired in November 1958. He died in Australia almost immediately afterwards.

The *Wanganella's* lifeboats were removed from the ship (below) while she was under repair in the dry dock; here they are being prepared for hoisting back on their davits. The liner is berthed at the floating dock mooring wharf; the dock with its crane can be seen behind her. She is sporting her new bow, its fresh paint contrasting with the rest of the hull which is soon to be repainted. [*Ian J. Farquhar collection*]

The original caption for this photo, taken on the *Wanganella's* starting platform, reads: 'Reason to feel proud. John Wylie, Chief Engineer, stands by the engine room telegraph (after) the bridge has ordered 'Full Ahead'.' The date is 8th December 1948 and the *Wanganella* is undergoing final engine trials at the conclusion of her repairs, prior to departing Wellington for Sydney with passengers the following day. [*Alexander Turnbull Library, Wellington, New Zealand. PICT-000090*]

Top right: Passengers disembarking from the *Wanganella* onto the Wellington Harbour Board's pilot launch *Arahina* early on the morning of Monday 20th January 1947, about eight or nine hours after the stranding. Fellow passengers crowd the rails to watch this unscheduled finale to their Tasman voyage. Note the damage already done to the paintwork along the *Wanganella's* hull from vessels coming alongside to take passengers off.

Middle right: The salvage tug *Terawhiti* alongside the *Wanganella*, taking mail bags aboard from the stranded liner.

Bottom right: The Wellington Harbour Board tug *Toia* standing by the *Wanganella* with towing wires made fast to the liner's stern, 6th February 1947. *Toia* is waiting for any indication the *Wanganella* may at last free herself from the reef as high tide and the compressors driving air into the forward holds take their effect.

Opposite page, top left; Salvage workers inspect the liner's hull from a rope ladder. Outer Rock is just below them.

Opposite page, top right: The top of the *Wanganella's* number two hold looking across to starboard. The hold has been sealed off with welded plates and these in turn have been reinforced with steel beams placed fore-and-aft across the hatch top. Drums of concrete and sacks filled with sand have then been placed on the hatch top to weigh it down. Gas cylinders for oxy-acetylene cutting torches lie in the foreground. Three very well-paid salvage workers pause in the sunshine to look up at the camera.

Opposite page, middle: The caption for this photo when it first appeared in newspapers in February 1947, reads: 'The last photograph of the *Wanganella* on Barrett Reef, Wellington. A view taken at about 6 pm on Thursday (6th February 1947). Three hours later the liner was freed from the reef, where she had been held fast for nearly 18 days.' Note how her bow has gone much deeper in the water as she slowly works clear of the rocks.

Opposite page, bottom: Repairs fully completed, the *Wanganella* is farewelled by well-wishers as she departs Queens Wharf in Wellington on her first sailing to Sydney, late afternoon on 9th December 1948. Note the two young ladies with berets, gloves and corporal's rank, third and fourth from left.

dock and across the harbour to Clyde Quay Wharf for completion of repairs.

The opportunity was now taken to do further work on refurbishing the *Wanganella's* interiors after her war service. The last of the drab green hospital paint was covered over. Visitors to the ship who remembered her from the 1930s now declared her public rooms to be as handsome as they had been when the *Wanganella* was new.

Sea trials were conducted in Cook Strait on 29th and 30th November 1948 with the tug *Toia* in attendance. Under the command of Captain H.F. Norrie, the *Wanganella* departed Queens Wharf for Sydney at 4.20 pm on 9th December 1948, fully booked with 409 passengers aboard. Over 1,000 people were at the wharf to say farewell. The liner had been out of service for 22 months. J. Wylie was again the *Wanganella's* Chief Engineer; he had been Chief on the night of the stranding and for her delivery voyage from Belfast 16 years earlier.

Court of Inquiry

Retribution came swiftly for Captain Darroch, who faced a Court of Inquiry in Wellington from 25th to 28th February 1947. The Court comprised A.M. Goulding, a Wellington magistrate, assisted by two marine assessors, Captains J. Rankine of Napier and A.T. Norton of Wellington.

In his defence, Captain Darroch asserted that the stranding had been caused by variations between the charts for Port Nicholson (Wellington Harbour) and Cook Strait, which had put the *Wanganella* a mile to the west of her proper course. Navigation lights at the harbour entrance also had not been flashing at their correct intervals on the night of 19th January. Captain Darroch further stated that after the stranding it had been found that armour plate, placed as ballast in the ship's number two 'tween decks hold in September 1946, had caused a deviation of eight degrees in the ship's compasses.

Giving evidence, Captain Darroch also told the court how what he described as 'peculiar' visibility on the night of 19th January 1947 had 'trapped' him and prevented his correctly identifying the lights ahead of the ship. 'It was not possible', he said, 'to see the shore at all and it was difficult to pick up dark objects in the water. It was also difficult to judge the distance from a buoy until you were right up to it'.

The court did not accept Captain Darroch's claims, all of which were refuted by expert witnesses. Captain Darroch was found to be in default for not having exercised sufficient caution when navigating his ship as he approached Wellington Harbour. Had the Master examined his charts more carefully, he

Captain Robert Darroch, the *Wanganella's* Master from December 1938 to February 1947, is seen on her bridge (left) just after she was towed off Barrett Reef and three weeks before he was relieved of command. To his very great credit he successfully brought the *Wanganella* through all the challenges and perils of her war service only to lose all in an act of carelessness off the south coast of Wellington on the night of 19th January 1947. Although the court of inquiry suspended his master's certificate for just three months, in those times such a penalty meant no major shipowner would employ him again. In his 74th year it seems he was still doing what he could to recover his good name, having gained a position as Master for one voyage aboard the 40-year-old motor coaster *Awahou*. She is shown in this photo (below), a humbling demotion for Captain Darroch after nine years in command of the *Wanganella*. In early September 1952 the *Awahou* set off from the Sydney wharves in good weather with general cargo for Lord Howe Island in mid-Tasman Sea. A garbled radio call believed have come from her was picked up in Adelaide on 10th September 1952, stating that she was to the north of Lord Howe Island and in distress. After that, and despite extensive searches, neither the *Awahou* nor her crew of 12 including Captain Darroch were ever seen again. *[Ian J. Farquhar collection]*

The *Wanganella* as she is so well remembered (above). In this photo she is berthed at Queens Wharf in Wellington, some time in the late 1940s or very early 1950s. A radar scanner on its tower has been added to the deckhouse just aft of the bridge, otherwise her appearance is unchanged following the liner's return to service in December 1948. On the promenade deck, white-painted canvas screens have been fitted to give shelter from the Tasman winds. These were replaced by windows during the *Wanganella's* refit at Sydney in 1952. *[V.H. Young and L.A. Sawyer]*

The *Wanganella* departing Wellington for Sydney on a chilly day in the late 1940s or early 1950s (right). All mooring lines have been let go and she is moving slow astern past the outer end of Queens Wharf. This photo by Vic Young captures the old-world atmosphere of sailing day; passengers thronging the rails, streamers linking them with the crowds on the wharf. Shouted good-byes, smells of fresh paint and funnel gases, the rumble of engines, telegraphs ringing on the bridge as the Master gives his orders. As always the *Wanganella* is immaculate. Note the steam whistle mounted on the side of her second funnel. *[V.H. Young and L.A. Sawyer]*

A marvellous shot of the *Wanganella* off Queens Wharf in Wellington (left), taken in March 1950. The ship is outbound for Sydney and passengers crowd her rails. She has just undocked without the aid of tugs. After letting go all lines aft, the *Wanganella's* head rope and spring have been used to warp her off the end of the berth. A steady north-westerly wind is assisting the liner's propellers in swinging her stern out. At the truck of the mainmast is the blue diagonal cross with red background of Huddart Parker's house flag. The dark-coated figure of the *Wanganella's* Master can be seen on the small platform outboard of the starboard wing cab, while her Chief Officer is at the rails just above the forecastle break. Soon she will go astern into the inner harbour, then turn for the run down to the harbour entrance and Cook Strait, where the liner will steer westwards for Australia three and a half days away. [V.H. Young and L.A. Sawyer]

Classic *Wanganella* (below). She is just getting underway in Auckland Harbour for the start of another Tasman crossing, streamers trailing in the breeze along her side. Note the additional windows installed on her first class promenade deck during the 1952 refit. The remaining side openings aft of the windows are shrouded in canvas screens in anticipation of gale force winds awaiting the ship in mid-Tasman Sea. [V.H. Young and L.A. Sawyer]

The *Wanganella's* exquisite first class dining saloon, photographed at Wellington in 1948. Located on C Deck forward in the ship, it had seating for 260 passengers and featured a lofty cross-vaulted dome. Concealed electric lighting was fitted behind lattice-glazed windows in the dome and along the sides of the room. *[Alexander Turnbull Library, Wellington, New Zealand. W. H. Raine Collection, 101225½]*

At the forward end of the *Wanganella's* promenade deck, facing the bow, was the first class lounge. This photograph was taken at Wellington in 1948, just before the liner resumed passenger sailings after nearly two years under repair. Decorated in a Spanish theme, panelled in veneered woods and with a central dome, the lounge's furnishings would have looked much the same 15 years later when the *Wanganella* arrived in Deep Cove. Once there, the lounge was turned into a bar for hundreds of workmen needing liquid solace after a long shift in the tailrace tunnel or cutting the mountain road over Wilmot Pass. Immediately aft of the lounge was the first class reading room and library. *[Alexander Turnbull Library, Wellington, New Zealand. W. H. Raine Collection, 101219½]*

Aft on the promenade deck was the first class smoking room together with a veranda area looking towards the *Wanganella's* stern. This photo, taken in 1948, shows the smoking room's port forward corner. Smoking or smoke rooms aboard liners from the era to which the *Wanganella* belonged were exclusively for male passengers. Here, gentlemen travelling first class could take their leisure while playing at cards, sipping their favourite aperitif or discussing the latest twists and turns of world politics. Deep leather chairs and dark timber panelling convey the smoking room's solid, masculine atmosphere. *[Alexander Turnbull Library, Wellington, New Zealand. New Zealand Free Lance Collection, PICT-000059]*

While the smoking room was the preserve of males, the smoking lounge next door was where their ladies and 'the younger set' could foregather (above and right). Its décor seems much lighter and more appealing. Upholstered settees have been added during the *Wanganella's* post-war refit. Like the *Wanganella's* other first class public rooms the smoking lounge had an elegant vaulted ceiling. At its forward end, shown at right, was an imposing marble fireplace. 'The walls are vellum-tinted,' says 'The Motor Ship' in its December 1932 coverage of the then-new *Wanganella*, 'and the round-headed windows are lattice-glazed. Tones of blue and ivory have been chosen for the furniture and the architraves of the doors are carved and treated in a similar manner.' Both the smoking room and smoking lounge were fitted out as bars once the ship was in Deep Cove. *[Alexander Turnbull Library, Wellington, New Zealand. New Zealand Free Lance Collection, PICT-000058 and PICT-000060)]*

would have realised the light he was steering for was not the southernmost or front leading light but, in fact, the buoy light marking Barrett Reef. In particular, the position of Pencarrow Light, clearly visible and located just south of the Barrett Reef Light on the other side of the entrance channel, should have alerted Captain Darroch to his error. If this light had been the front leading light, as he believed, then Pencarrow Light should have been well astern as he came towards the leading light, and not off his starboard quarter.

Noting its 'extreme regret' in view of Captain Darroch's long and otherwise exemplary record, the court suspended his master's certificate for three months. No other officer or member of the *Wanganella's* crew was blamed. The inquiry did not call into question any part of Captain Darroch's conduct during the evacuation of passengers or salvage of the ship from Barrett Reef.

Captain Darroch left the *Wanganella* immediately and returned to Australia. It was a

humiliating end to a very long and distinguished career with Huddart Parker, Captain Darroch having served with the company since 1904 entirely without mishap. Perhaps after having successfully commanded the *Wanganella* through all the many demands and dangers of wartime, Captain Darroch's confidence in his navigation skills had reached a point where entering Wellington Harbour in fine, clear weather was a task he saw as entirely straightforward for a master of his experience. By his own admission at the Court of Inquiry, he had not been into Wellington for three or four years, reason enough to have given closer attention to the charts and even to have requested the services of a Wellington Harbour Board pilot. (Use of pilots was not compulsory at the time for ships entering and leaving Wellington Harbour.)

Captain Darroch went back to sea. He was Master of the 407 ton, 40-year-old motor coaster *Awahou* when she was lost in the Tasman Sea with

This photo, showing all the detail of her upper decks, is arguably the finest broadside shot of the *Wanganella* ever taken. Ian Farquhar is the camera man and he is on the bridge of the *Brisbane Star* (11,076/1937) at Auckland in October 1952. The liner is passing the *Brisbane Star* having just arrived in port. Note how the additional windows fitted to the first class promenade deck did not replicate the original nine windows under the bridge house at the forward end of this deck. *[Ian J. Farquhar collection]*

Sailing day; a fine, sunny afternoon in Wellington Harbour during the late 1950s. The flag of Australia flies in the north westerly breeze from the gaff on the *Wanganella's* mainmast as she gathers way after having just departed Queens Wharf. This view shows the enlarged deckhouse at the liner's stern, added during her post-war refit to provide improved crew accommodation. The upper level of this deckhouse was later extended right to the *Wanganella's* stern. Her bow is pointing towards Eastbourne on the eastern shores of Wellington Harbour, while behind her is Oriental Bay. *[Alexander Turnbull Library, Wellington New Zealand. W. Hall Raine collection, F20840¼]*

The *Wanganella* underway in Sydney Harbour, viewed from the Sydney Harbour Bridge. *[J. and M. Clarkson collection]*

all hands on 10th September 1952. The *Awahou* had been on passage from Sydney to Lord Howe Island with cargo, Captain Darroch having been engaged as relieving master for one voyage.

The cost of the *Wanganella's* stranding was considerable. Towage and salvage fees for getting the ship off Barrett Reef amounted to £60,000 with a further £300,000 spent on repairs and dock charges. By comparison, the cost in 1947 of building a replacement for the *Wanganella* was approximately £1,500,000. Each of the 18 crew members who had worked aboard the ship while she was on Barrett Reef had been paid £324 in wages, a total of £5,832. And on top of these costs was the loss of business earnings for Huddart Parker during the almost two years the *Wanganella* had been out of service.

Tasman twilight

The 1950s passed uneventfully for the *Wanganella*. Now into her third decade, she was a popular ship and a familiar sight at the wharves of Sydney, Auckland and Wellington Harbours. The liner maintained her owner's weekly sailings between Sydney and either Wellington or Auckland on alternate weeks, in tandem with the Union Company's *Monowai*. During a major refit in 1952 the windows of the *Wanganella's* first class promenade deck were extended aft almost to the end of the promenade deck. It was reported that, as part of this refit, Huddart Parker seriously considered removing the *Wanganella's* forward dummy funnel and

mounting part of it on top of her second funnel. Doing so would, it was hoped, alleviate the problem of funnel smoke polluting the ship's upper decks. The idea was not implemented and she kept her twin funnel profile to the end of her life. Later, the upper level of the ship's poop deckhouse was extended right to the stern to provide a new recreation room for stewards. The changes did nothing for her already cluttered looks.

The *Wanganella's* public rooms were refurbished in 1955-56 along with some of her cabin accommodation. In April 1958 her bow was once again seriously damaged, this time while she was being manoeuvred into Cockatoo Island dockyard at Sydney. Repairs took ten days. During the winter of that year the *Wanganella* undertook a series of cruises, being replaced on Huddart Parker's trans-Tasman service by the company's *Westralia*. These cruises took her up to the warmth of the South Pacific islands while in summer the *Wanganella* cruised the southern fjords of New Zealand, just as she had in the 1930s. Passengers filled the ship for these trips not only because of the scenery and relaxation but also the well-known excellence of the *Wanganella's* dining rooms. By 1960 passenger capacity was 292 first class and 108 second with 48 interchangeable between either class. The *Wanganella's* crew numbered 150.

Commercial airliner travel was growing rapidly between Australia and New Zealand and on 31st May 1960 the *Monowai*, then 35 years old, was withdrawn. The *Wanganella* continued on her own.

Over three decades since her launch, the *Wanganella* looks smart, business-like and far from retirement as she moves under the Sydney Harbour Bridge, from where this photo was taken by John Mathieson in 1962. She is in her short-lived McIlwraith McEacharn funnel colours. Her cluttered yet beautifully maintained upper decks must have occupied a small army of seamen in an endless cycle of washing, scraping and painting. Note the top of the forward funnel, which was a dummy. *[John Mathieson]*

In the meantime Huddart Parker Ltd. had been sold to Bitumen and Oil Refineries (Aust) Ltd. in September 1961, and on 27th October the company's new owner sold all of Huddart Parker's ships, including the *Wanganella*, to McIlwraith McEacharn Ltd. of Melbourne. The liner was taken over by her new owner at Sydney on 1st November. The *Wanganella's* buff funnels were repainted in McIlwraith, McEacharn's red and black livery. She resumed trans-Tasman sailings with her passenger and cargo business being managed for her owner by the Union Steam Ship Company.

On 26th March 1962, while in mid-Tasman on passage from Sydney to Auckland, the number four piston rod of the *Wanganella's* port engine fractured. The broken rod fell into the crank case where it was struck by the rotating crank. This in turn resulted in the piston being driven out through the crank case, fracturing the engine bedplate casting. After a delay in Auckland the liner returned with passengers to Sydney on one engine, arriving there on 4th April. She was out of service until 2nd May while repairs were made. Perhaps with understandable haste McIlwraith, McEacharn announced only three days later that it had sold the *Wanganella* after owning her for just 289 days. The decision seemed well justified when on the morning of 12th June 1962, while manoeuvring in

Sydney Harbour at the end of a Tasman crossing, the *Wanganella* suffered a major engine room explosion. Her engines had been stopped but, on going astern, the starting air valve on one cylinder jammed open. When the cylinder fired, hot combustion gas passed into the starting air line, igniting a quantity of oil residue. No casualties are known to have been reported.

Repairs lasted five days until 17th June 1962. On 25th July, under the command of Captain William Uttley, the *Wanganella* reached Sydney at the end of her final trans-Tasman voyage. She was dry docked and de-stored and her crew paid off prior to the ship being laid up in Sydney to await her new owner, the Hang Fung Shipping and Trading Co. Ltd. of Hong Kong.

Change of ownership took place on 15th August 1962. Hang Fung planned to use its new acquisition for a service between Australia and Hong Kong and so on 25th August the *Wanganella* departed Sydney for Hong Kong, still wearing her McIlwraith McEacharn funnel colours. Her name was not altered but Hong Kong was now her port of registry. By 27th October, her funnels repainted black with two silver bands, she was in Auckland for a cruise to Melbourne, taking horse racing enthusiasts there for the running of the Melbourne Cup. Under the command of Captain F. Simpson and manned by 36 European officers and a Chinese crew of 120, she next began a

On 17th October 1961, 29 years after she had been purchased by Huddart Parker, the company's new owner sold the *Wanganella* to McIlwraith McEacharn Ltd., another well-known Australian shipping company. Founded in London in 1875 by two Scotsmen, Andrew McIlwraith and Malcolm McEacharn, the company ran passenger and cargo services between the coastal ports of Australia. Most notable among their ships was the splendid motor liner *Kanimbla* of 1936. In this photo the *Wanganella*, her funnels repainted in her new owner's black and red livery, is dressed overall with flags most probably to mark her acquisition by McIlwraith McEacharn. They kept her for little more than six months. *[Ships in Focus]*

44

Thirty two years old and still looking splendid. The *Wanganella* in Hang Fung funnel colours, setting out for a cruise from Brisbane on 21st April 1963. Streamers fly from her decks and the sun glints off fresh hull paint beneath her name. She is nearing the end of her seagoing life; in just a few months she will be laid up in Sydney and offered for sale. In August, four months after this photo was taken, the *Wanganella* left Australian waters for the final time, sold to Utah Construction and Mining and bound for Deep Cove in New Zealand. *[V.H. Young and L.A. Sawyer]*

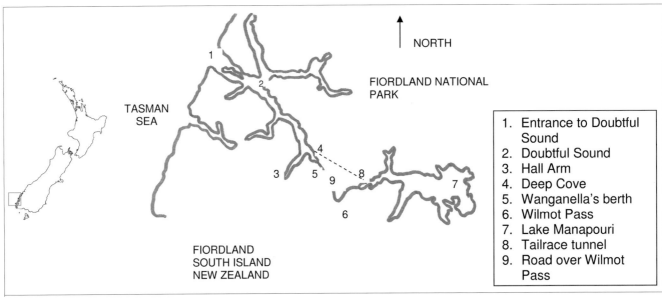

Deep Cove and Doubtful Sound in the South Island of New Zealand.

1. Entrance to Doubtful Sound
2. Doubtful Sound
3. Hall Arm
4. Deep Cove
5. Wanganella's berth
6. Wilmot Pass
7. Lake Manapouri
8. Tailrace tunnel
9. Road over Wilmot Pass

series of one-class cruises to the Pacific Islands and Australian ports. In November 1962 the *Wanganella* was berthed at Fremantle as a floating hotel for the 1962 Perth Commonwealth Games. Further cruises were scheduled up until January 1964. It was reported in 1962 that she had been chartered to an Auckland venture known as Anglo-Japanese Steam Ship Navigation Ltd. for a passenger service from New Zealand to Japan. Ambitiously, given her now less-than-dependable engines, this service to Yokohama and Osaka was to be routed via Sydney, Noumea, Manila and Hong Kong. There were also reports of cruises from Sydney to destinations as far away as Tahiti and Brazil. Swimming pools, sun decks and new tapered funnels were to be added to the ship.

Deep Cove

Nothing came of any of this. After a few more cruises in 1963 the *Wanganella* was laid up in Sydney and offered for sale. On 20th August that year she departed Sydney and Australian waters for the last time. At 32 years of age she could expect a scrap yard as her next destination but there was to be one final, memorable role for the veteran liner.

In New Zealand work was about to start on the Manapouri Power Project. This involved building a hydro-electric power station inside a huge underground cavern, to be excavated from solid rock 200 metres below Lake Manapouri in the South Island. Water would descend to the power station's turbines from the lake, then leave via a tailrace tunnel 10.65 kilometres in length. This tunnel would run westwards below the Southern Alps, emptying into Deep Cove at the head of Doubtful Sound on the west coast of the South Island.

Deep Cove was to be the *Wanganella's* home for the next six and a half years. She had been purchased by Utah Construction and Mining, a United States firm that was part of the consortium contracted

to build the tailrace tunnel. Work was to proceed from the Deep Cove end of the tunnel, but in 1963 Deep Cove was one of the most remote and inaccessible places in New Zealand. Surrounded by untouched mountain and forest wilderness, it was a broad, steep-sided, deep-water inlet at the south-eastern extremity of Doubtful Sound, 35 kilometres from the open sea. There were no roads into or around Deep Cove and a small trampers' lodge the only human habitation.

Still wearing her black and silver Hang Fung funnel colours, the *Wanganella* crossed the Tasman Sea with a crew of 34, 26 of whom were Chinese. She called at Auckland before heading south and entering Doubtful Sound on 29th August 1963. Earlier the Royal New Zealand Navy had surveyed and marked a passage up the Sound for the *Wanganella* and for the many ships that would follow her, delivering supplies and the heavy machinery needed for tunnel construction.

Initially the *Wanganella* was anchored off the entrance to Hall Arm, just west of Deep Cove. Using the ship's lifeboats, workers brought in by float plane went ashore and began sinking bolts into the high, tree-shrouded cliffs to take heavy steel mooring lines. On 3rd September 1963 the *Wanganella* weighed anchor and came into Deep Cove, turning so that her bow pointed back towards the Cove's entrance. She was secured to a temporary berth just off the cliffs in what became known as 'Wanganella Cove', a small bay on the south side of Deep Cove nearest its head.

This was the very last time during her long life that the *Wanganella* was moved by her propellers. From this point she ceased to be an ocean-going passenger liner as her conversion to a floating workers' hostel began in earnest. Up to 550 men would be employed on the tunnel and on building a 22 kilometre road from Deep Cove over the mountainous Wilmot Pass to Lake Manapouri. They would be accommodated aboard the ship and in rows of huts later constructed next to the *Wanganella's* berth.

Everything not wanted for her new role was either taken ashore and burnt or simply thrown over the side. Included in this was the *Wanganella's* radio equipment and the contents of her printing shop. The ship's hospital was enlarged, her barber's shop became a post and telegram office with resident postmaster, and a police constable was appointed with his own on-board police station. The purser's bureau forward on A Deck was turned into an office for the hostel manager, R. Lynch, who was in charge of the ship.

The first class cabins on A Deck were occupied by the tunnel project manager and his executive staff. Further aft, offices and accommodation were built into the *Wanganella's* second class promenade deck for staff from Bechtel Corporation, the American firm engaged by the New Zealand Government to design and oversee the Manapouri Power Project. The ship's library was retained while one of her lower holds was converted into a gymnasium. No longer would there be white-jacketed waiters and genteel table service in either of the *Wanganella's* two dining rooms. Both

were now to cater for round-the-clock shift work once tunnelling operations got underway, managers and workers lining up for their meals and eating together. Most important of all, the *Wanganella's* first class lounge, smoking lounge and smoking room on her promenade deck were fitted out as bars for the colossal thirsts that tunnel and road building would produce. The *Wanganella* was to become notorious for its drinking culture.

Before tunnelling could start, the first task was to clear the forest around the shore where the *Wanganella* was moored and where the tunnel entrance was to be located. Gangs of workers were landed in the ship's boats each morning, returning to the ship when work finished for the day. Their labours were hampered by prodigious rainfall, the rugged muddy terrain and by endless sandflies. Near the *Wanganella*, blasting of the steep bluffs commenced. The ship's upper decks were damaged slightly by falling rock from this work. Cutting and excavation went on throughout 1964; by 1965 a level platform had been

This photo is dated 30th September 1963. The *Wanganella* lies moored in Deep Cove, having arrived there four weeks previously. Although it will be over six years before she feels the open sea again, the *Wanganella* still looks every bit the ocean-going passenger liner. Utah Construction and Mining, her new American owner, soon began reducing her to a charmless floating barracks and tavern. The launch alongside the *Wanganella* was named *Miss Akaroa* and was one of a number of tenders that served the ship during her time in Deep Cove. The ship's boats are being used to ferry workers ashore where construction of the tailrace tunnel has started. *[Alexander Turnbull Library, Wellington New Zealand. Dominion Post Collection, EP/1963/3168]*

formed just above the water's edge. This was to be the *Wanganella's* permanent berth at Deep Cove for the next five years; in early 1965 she was winched into place. Two cantilevered bridges, one forward and one aft, linked her to the shore and a connecting road was built to the nearby site of the tunnel entrance.

Tunnelling went on 24 hours a day. Alongside the *Wanganella* ships came and went, bringing fuel, mail and the six tons of food required each week, swung aboard using her derricks. The ship retained her Hang Fung funnel colours and was kept well maintained, but her external decks were soon cluttered with temporary sheds and buildings large and small, all to provide extra accommodation and give protection from the constant rain. Largest among them was a three storey building erected over the *Wanganella's* number three hatch, aft of the main superstructure. The big deckhouse at the ship's stern had another level added to it. Stairs with a walkway protruding out from the ship's port side were built to link these structures with the *Wanganella's* boat deck. On the boat deck itself, all lifeboats and their davits were removed. Sheds even appeared on the monkey island and on the *Wanganella's* bridge wings.

Accounts tell of a very happy atmosphere among the tunnellers, tradesmen, engineers and labourers from countries all over the world who lived aboard and alongside the 'Wanga', as they called her. A number of them were men on the run from their wives or from justice, having changed their names to hide their true identities. Often the police constable aboard the ship suspected the truth as to their backgrounds, but opted not to confront them as long as there was no trouble. For those with distant homes and families the almost total isolation of Deep Cove meant the arrival of mail took on great significance. This was flown across the mountains by seaplane from Invercargill and the port of Bluff, located at the southern end of the South Island. In addition to distributing mail, the ship's postmaster was responsible for the single telephone line that connected the ship with the outside world. This line ran up over Wilmot Pass from the *Wanganella*, hung from tree branches where often it was cut by ice, felled by winds or buried in snow.

Saturday was always the biggest night aboard the *Wanganella*. The workers devised concerts and held sing-alongs accompanied by pianists among them on the ship's grand piano. Apart from the nurses who staffed the hospital, it was an all-male environment. There is no record of what they made of the faded elegance of the *Wanganella's* public rooms, the Spanish and Italian decoration so out of place amid the mists and chill rainfall of Deep Cove. Doubtless the furnishings occasioned little if any pause in the urgent business of slaking thirsts and appetites after a hard day's tunnelling and road building. Nor the equally serious work of following the horses, a pastime that, in those days, enjoyed a huge following in New Zealand. On race days the most crowded place

Above 'Wanganella Cove', photographed on 13th April 1965 from a circling aircraft. Two ramps secure the *Wanganella* to her permanent berth, into which she was moved early in 1965. The forward ramp appears to be still under construction. Some of her port side lifeboats remain in place; these will soon be removed as more structures are added to her upper decks to provide further accommodation. The narrow rock platform against which the liner is berthed was cut by explosives and jack hammers from the cliff sides of Deep Cove. It was subsequently widened by further blasting, the *Wanganella* being hauled off the land while this work was underway.

The photo shows that, at the time when it was taken, waste water from the *Wanganella* was discharged straight into Deep Cove, where it can be seen pooling around the ship. *[Alexander Turnbull Library, Wellington, New Zealand. EP-Ships-Wanganella-04]*

aboard the *Wanganella* was the betting shop. Darts tournaments were also held, movies were screened and a newspaper called 'The Wangatella' published on board.

The *Wanganella* did not leave Deep Cove during the six and a half years she was employed on the Manapouri Power Project. Despite ships as large as a 20,000 ton tanker calling at Deep Cove, hers must have been one of the world's most solitary anchorages, far from the open sea, enclosed by towering, snow-capped mountains and with vast, ancient forests on all sides. One writer has told how, during the day, the *Wanganella* often seemed almost deserted. But at night she became an oasis of lights and sound, her bars filled to their noisiest capacity and her decks thronged with people as if it were sailing time and she was back at the docks of Sydney or Wellington.

This photo well conveys the lonely but spectacular natural setting for the *Wanganella's* last assignment in her long life. Here she is at her permanent berth at the head of Deep Cove, the forward cantilevered bridge visible at her bow over which trucks came and went with supplies (including, most importantly, vast quantities of bottled beer). Ahead of the ship at lower right is the crude structure where vessels tied up while delivering cement and other materials for the tailrace tunnel's construction. *[Ian J. Farquhar collection]*

Deep Cove a year or two after the aerial photograph of the *Wanganella* was taken (previous page), showing part of the forest and towering mountain wilderness that was her home from 3rd September 1963 to 17th April 1970. The somewhat flimsy ramps linking the ship with the shore were later replaced with much heavier cantilevered steel bridges roofed over from the weather. Note the variety of sheds and buildings added to the *Wanganella*, particularly at her stern. Seagulls that have flown a long way inland from the sea are lined up on one of the mooring wires off the ship's bow, in anticipation of lunchtime scraps from the *Wanganella's* kitchens. *[Newall Dunn collection]*

The road over Wilmot Pass was completed in September 1965 and 'hole-through' of the tailrace tunnel occurred on 22nd October 1968. By 1970 the work force at Deep Cove had departed and only a caretaker plus a handful of others were left aboard the *Wanganella*. Utah Construction and Mining sold her in December 1969 to the New Zealand Government who in turn sold her to the Australia Pacific Shipping Company of Hong Kong, one of eleven companies which tendered for the purchase of the ship. The new owner planned to restore her for use as a passenger liner. The *Wanganella* was prepared for sea, her anchors being raised with some difficulty after having been on the bottom of Deep Cove at a depth of nearly 1,000 feet for over six years. She left Deep Cove bound for

Her duties as an accommodation ship over, the *Wanganella* is towed away from Deep Cove on 17th April 1970 by the Dutch tug *Barentz Zee*. *[Ian J. Farquhar collection]*

Hong Kong on 17th April 1970, under tow by the Dutch tug *Barentz Zee* (526/1957), which had arrived in Deep Cove on 8th April after towing a dredge from Antwerp to Sydney. The trip through Doubtful Sound to the open sea took five hours. For what was to be her penultimate voyage the *Wanganella's* crew comprised three men equipped with a butane gas stove for cooking and torches for light.

Local stories have it that during her years at Deep Cove a vast under-sea mountain of empty beer cans and bottles accumulated beneath the old ship's keel. Apparently she had to be dragged free of this before she could leave. Whatever intentions her new owner had for the *Wanganella*, once in Hong Kong it was soon found that her engines would need to be

fully replaced if she was ever to put to sea again under her own power. Without further delay she was sold once more, this time to Taiwanese shipbreakers. The *Wanganella* was towed to Kaohsiung, arriving there on 5th June 1970 seven weeks after leaving Deep Cove and nearly 41 years after her launch in Belfast. She was demolished by Shyeh Sheng Fuat Steel and Iron Works.

Deep Cove is part of Fiordland National Park in New Zealand and so, with the tailrace tunnel completed, extensive work was done to clean up and restore the area fully to its natural beauty. The *Wanganella's* berth is still there but, like the old lady herself, the once thriving frontier town of which she was hub has now passed into history

The end. Dated 23rd June 1970, this is perhaps the very last photo taken of the *Wanganella*. Empty and silent, she lies at Kaohsiung, Taiwan, waiting to be broken up having left Deep Cove under tow 67 days earlier. The photo shows to good effect the various structures her US owners added to the ship's upper decks during her sojourn at Deep Cove, all to provide extra accommodation and keep out the incessant rain. The poop deckhouse has an extra level and the upper two floors of the large building placed over the number three hatch can be seen just forward of the *Wanganella's* mainmast. The ship's boats have long gone and a lean-to has been installed over the monkey island above the wheelhouse. *[V.H. Young and L.A. Sawyer]*

General arrangement drawings of *Wanganella*

These drawings depict the ship after she had been modified to Huddart Parker's requirements: they show more detail that those that were drawn up when the ship had been completed as the *Achimota*. [*Ulster Folk and Transport Museum*]

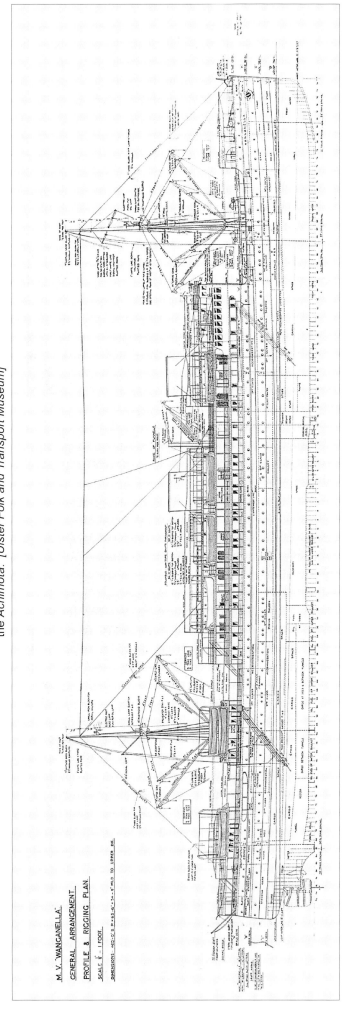

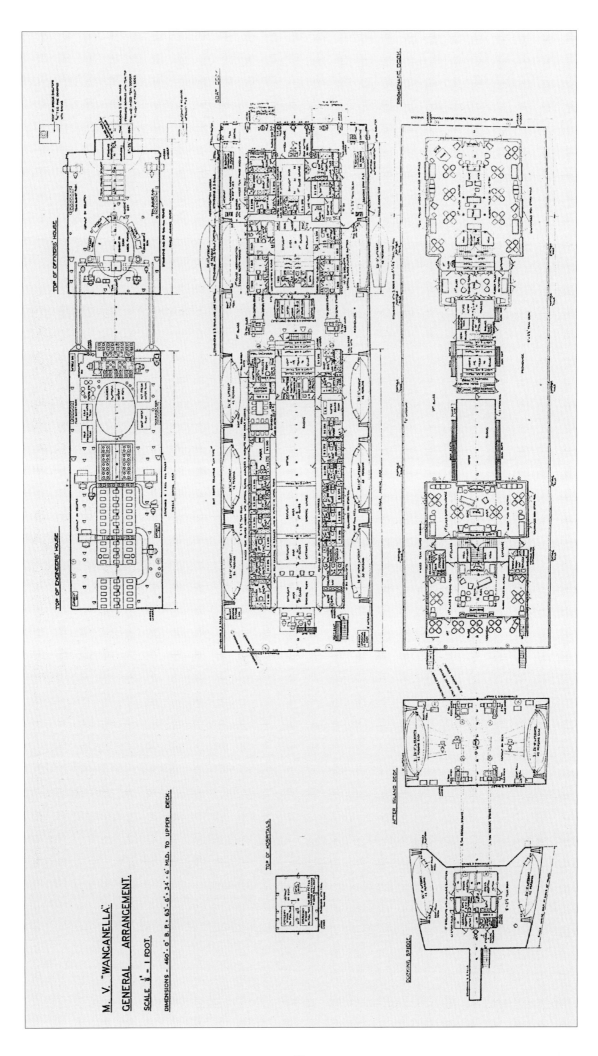

M. V. "WANGANELLA"

GENERAL ARRANGEMENT.

SCALE $\frac{1}{8}$" = 1 FOOT.

DIMENSIONS - 460'·0" B.P. × 63'·6'·34'·6' MLD. TO UPPER DECK.

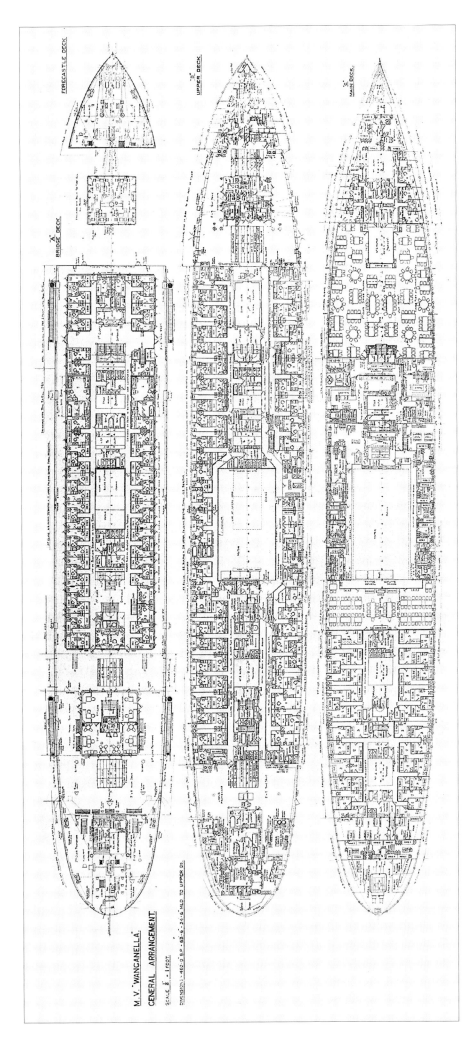

M.V. 'WANGANELLA'
GENERAL ARRANGEMENT

SCALE ⅛" = 1 FOOT

DIMENSIONS 460'0 B.P. × 63'6 × 34'6 MLD TO UPPER DK

FORECASTLE DECK

'B' UPPER DECK

'C' MAIN DECK

'A' BRIDGE DECK

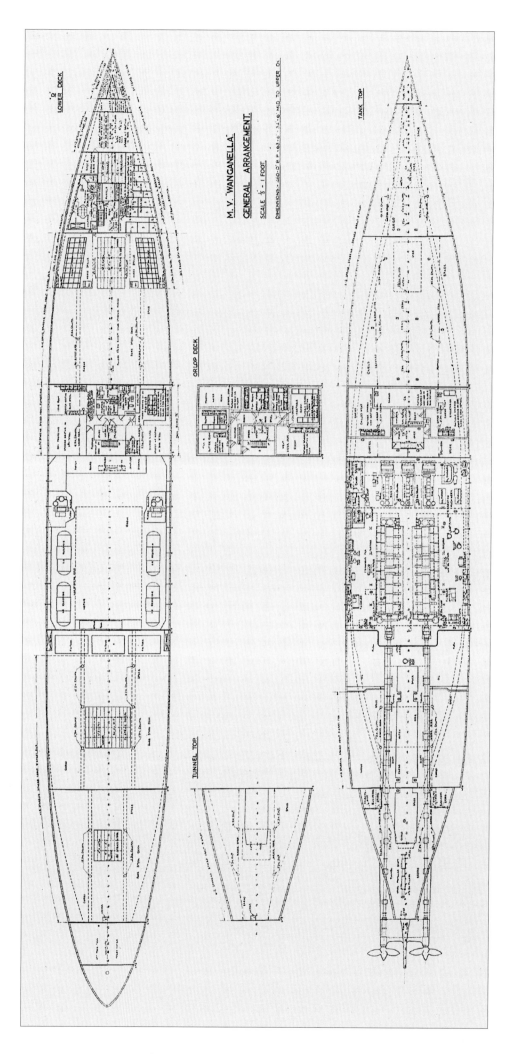

M. V. 'WANGANELLA'

GENERAL ARRANGEMENT.

SCALE ⅜" = 1 FOOT

BOATS THAT FLY

In their day the *Wanganella* and the *Monowai* provided the best of cuisine and comfort but even the *Monowai's* relatively high speed of 19 knots could not answer the growing demand for faster travel between Australia and New Zealand. The matchless *Awatea* with her 21-22 knot service speed provided that answer during the last halcyon years before the Second World War. How the directors of the Union Steam Ship Company, contemplating their gins and tonic after board meetings in the post-war years, must have lamented her loss. Wisely in hindsight they did not build a replacement liner, but kept the *Monowai* operating until 1960. The Union Company knew, much earlier than many of its shipping industry contemporaries, that its passenger clientele would soon take to the skies in ever-increasing numbers.

The long careers of *Wanganella* and the *Monowai* as passenger liners spanned in full the development of air travel across the Tasman, from nothing when they arrived at the start of the 1930s to regular commercial airliner flights every few days by the mid-1950s. Having seen it coming, the Union Company had sought a role for itself in this new industry. Masterminded by N.S. Falla, its visionary Managing Director, the Union Company in 1935 established a wholly-owned subsidiary, Union Airways of New Zealand Ltd. By coincidence, in 1936 both the Union Company and Huddart Parker each became one third shareholders in Australian National Airways with the Tasmanian Holyman dynasty, to be later joined as shareholders by The Adelaide Steamship Company and the Orient Line.

Regular passenger flights across the Tasman Sea had their beginning on 27th December 1937 when Imperial Airways' flying boat G-ADUT *Centaurus*, piloted by Captain J.W. Burgess, landed in Auckland Harbour after a 9 hour 10 minute journey from Sydney. Built by Short Brothers, the four-engined *Centaurus* was one of their C Class aircraft known as 'Empire boats'. *Centaurus* was the first commercial, passenger-carrying flying boat to visit Australia and New Zealand, doing so as part of a trans-world flight from Southampton to demonstrate the possibilities of linking the Empire by air travel. Following the success of this venture, and with Imperial Airways taking the lead, Tasman Empire Airways Ltd., known as TEAL, was founded in April 1940 jointly with Qantas and Union Airways. Their intention was to operate a flying boat service across the Tasman as a final leg to the Southampton to Sydney route.

Two new Short S30 C Class Empire flying boats, each able to carry 19 passengers, were ordered and paid for by Union Airways at the instigation of N.S. Falla. The first of these, ZK-AMA *Aotearoa*, reached Auckland after a twelve-day flight from

England via Sydney on 28th August 1939, just before war was declared with Germany. *Aotearoa* was piloted by the same Captain J.W. Burgess who had flown the *Centaurus* on its pioneering flight to New Zealand 20 months earlier. TEAL's second flying boat, ZK-AMC *Awarua*, arrived in Auckland on 3rd April 1940 at the end of her delivery flight from Poole, England, under the command of Captain Oscar Garden. The *Awarua's* First Officer, C.G. Griffiths, later became the best known of all the flying boat pilots who flew the Tasman skies.

With these two aircraft and under the management of Union Airways, TEAL ran the only passenger service of any type between Australia and New Zealand during the war years. The service was officially opened on 30th April 1940 when *Aotearoa* flew the 1,342 miles from Auckland to Sydney with nine passengers in just under nine hours. Cruising speed was 165 mph and the fare per passenger was NZ£30, a considerable sum at the time. Among the 31 bags of mail on board for the return flight was the first mail to travel exclusively by air from Great Britain to New Zealand. Regular air travel now began across the Tasman, flights taking between seven and eleven hours depending on wind conditions, usually leaving Rose Bay in Sydney at 4 am so that the crossing could be made in daylight, then landing at Auckland's Mechanic's Bay flying boat terminal by early to mid-afternoon. On average, six return flights a month were made.

Almost with a sense of glee, Qantas's Managing Director Hudson Fysh relates how, in the event of engine trouble over the Tasman, the flying boats could be lightened by jettisoning mail and passengers' luggage. The realities of this became all too apparent after the *Aotearoa* and *Awarua* were replaced 1946-47 with what were supposed to be improved aircraft. When withdrawn from service on 5th November 1947 the *Aotearoa* had crossed the Tasman 442 times in seven and a half years, flying a total of 1,230,000 miles. She was brought ashore at Mission Bay in Auckland and used as a tea room while the *Awarua* was broken up for scrap. Their replacements were four wartime Sunderland flying boats acquired by TEAL through the British Ministry of Supply. Converted to accommodate 30 passengers on two decks and fitted with new engines, they were known as Short S25 Sandringham Mark IV flying boats belonging to the Tasman Class. Named *Tasman*, *Australia*, *Auckland* and *New Zealand*, the Sandringhams were soon found to be under-powered.

On 7th December 1947 at 5.30 am, ZK-AME *New Zealand* departed Sydney for Auckland with 29 passengers. Three hours later, flying below 500 feet in

ZK-AMA *Aotearoa*, one of the two Short S30 C Class Empire flying boats which maintained the trans-Tasman air service during the Second World War. Throughout those years this aircraft and ZK-AMC *Awarua*, an identical machine, were the only regular link for people needing to travel between Australia and New Zealand. In this photo, taken during the war years, *Aotearoa* has been hauled ashore at Mechanics Bay, the flying boat terminal on Auckland Harbour, New Zealand. For the crowd of spectators in the foreground, the flying boat up close must have seemed enormous. Most of them would not have been near aircraft much bigger than a Tiger Moth biplane. *[Alexander Turnbull Library, Wellington, New Zealand. F–47827-½]*

bad weather, an oil leak was observed from the inner starboard engine. When the engine began smoking and vibrating, pilot Captain I. Patterson quickly feathered the propeller and turned back for Sydney. But the flying boat began losing height and ten minutes later was just 50 feet above the wave tops. An SOS message was radioed: 'Unable to maintain height. May have to land in the sea.' Passengers were ordered into lifejackets. First the crew's luggage was thrown overboard to try and lighten the aircraft and keep it airborne. Then the passengers' luggage and freight went out the door; *New Zealand* fortunately was carrying no mail. The flying boat now managed to get back to 100 feet but hit a rain squall and was soon just above the waves again. But once the squall had passed her pilots succeeded in getting the aircraft up to 1,000 feet, where she was met by two other flying boats and escorted back to Sydney.

Such was the impact of this near-disaster that in New Zealand a Royal Commission was established to investigate its causes. The commission's report, made public on 30th April 1948, criticised the issuing of airworthiness certificates in Britain for aircraft that

were to be used in the very different flying conditions found on the opposite side of the world in the Tasman Sea. Meanwhile, the four Sandringhams were withdrawn for modification from February to mid-June 1948. Once returned to service there were no further problems but the flying boats were kept only until new aircraft became available.

In November 1949 the Sandringhams were replaced by four much more successful Short S45A Mark IV Solent flying boats, each with 44 passenger seats on two decks. Able to operate at a much faster cruising speed of 244 mph and with a range of 3,000 miles, the Solents could fly to New Zealand and back to Sydney in one day. Named *Ararangi*, *Aotearoa II*, *Awatere* and *Aranui* (a fifth aircraft, *Aparima*, was added later) they made eight return crossings each week, four between Sydney and Auckland and four between Sydney and Wellington where a new flying boat terminal, at Evans Bay, was opened in October 1950. The 1,391-mile flight from Evans Bay to Sydney's Rose Bay took seven hours 30 minutes, then seven hours to return. The Solents offered excellent in-flight hospitality and at the time were seen as a

A Short S45A Mk IV Solent flying boat taking off from Evans Bay in Wellington Harbour, New Zealand on 3rd October 1950, bound for Sydney. This was the day the new terminal at Evans Bay was opened. Fully loaded, the flying boat required a run of about 900 yards to get airborne. Last and best of the trans-Tasman flying boats, the 35-ton Solents were manufactured by Short Brothers and Harland Ltd. at their Belfast works in Northern Ireland. Powered by four Bristol Hercules air-cooled piston engines developing a total of 7,760 hp for take-off, the Solents carried 44 passengers and a crew of eight: two pilots (captain and first officer), flight engineer, navigator, radio officer and three stewards or stewardesses. *[Archives New Zealand/ Te Rua Mahara o Te Kāwanatanga, Wellington Office, New Zealand. Photographer: W. Walker. Alexander Turnbull Library F20523-½ (AAQT 6401, A21134)]*

most glamorous way to travel, preferred by the rich, the famous and the important. Photographers and newspaper men often were on hand for departures and arrivals. But as with all the earlier flying boats the Solents' cabins were not pressurised. Often unable to fly above the rough weather encountered on the Tasman crossing, passengers in addition to fine clothes and fine tastes also needed strong stomachs.

In 1941 *Aotearoa* and *Awarua*, first of the flying boats, carried a total of 1,460 passengers, 14,200 pounds of cargo and 77,587 pounds of mail on 130 flights. By comparison, in 1951, the flying boats' biggest year when there was a prolonged waterfront strike in New Zealand, the Solents carried 39,621 passengers, 1,512,944 pounds of cargo and 632,892 pounds of mail on 1,215 flights.

The days of the flying boats were always numbered as the development of land-based commercial aircraft leapt ahead. Because Wellington at the time had no suitable airfield, TEAL's flying boat service continued into Wellington until the last flight departed there for Sydney on 25th June 1954. In March that year TEAL began a twice-weekly service from Christchurch to Sydney and a weekly service to Melbourne, using Douglas DC6 airliners. They were bigger and faster, crossing the Tasman in under six hours, and they were pressurised, enabling them to fly in smooth air above the turbulence. Auckland to Melbourne was added in 1957 and Auckland to Brisbane in 1959. The DC6s were replaced by Lockheed L188 turbo-prop aircraft from 1959. These airliners began direct flights to Australia from Wellington's new Rongotai Airport, which opened on 25th October 1959.

TEAL had continued to be managed by Union Airways, subsidiary of the Union Steam Ship Company, until the New Zealand government nationalised TEAL in April 1946. When TEAL set up its own administration Union Airways' role on the Tasman came to an end. It was not long before the Union Company's sea passenger operations ended too, killed off by the same air competition it had helped pioneer in 1940. Although the *Monowai* had enjoyed near-capacity sailings during her final year, she was 35 years old by 1960 and her demise had long been planned. To the *Wanganella* fell the distinction of being the very last passenger ship regularly crossing the Tasman Sea. When she reached Sydney on 25th July 1962 the airliners had the Tasman to themselves.

Maritime *tour de force*. Dressed overall with Sydney Harbour Bridge behind her, the brand new *Awatea* turns into Sydney Cove on her maiden arrival in Australia, Friday morning 18th September 1936. *[J. and M. Clarkson collection]*

AWATEA - THE TASMAN DESTROYER

Famous, fabulous, never to be forgotten: no account of the Tasman crossing would be entire without telling of the Union Steam Ship Company's *Awatea*. Over four triumphant years from September 1936 to July 1940 this magnificent ship bestrode the Tasman route, her speed, style and luxury unequalled. Acknowledged as the finest ship ever built for the Union Steam Ship Company, the *Awatea*'s life was tragically cut short in 1942, depriving her owner of its only modern international passenger vessel.

The 527.3 feet long, 13,482 gross register tonnage *Awatea* (meaning 'broad daylight' in the Maori language) came into existence as a result of the tenacity and leadership of N. S. Falla, who was appointed Managing Director of the Union Steam Ship Company in late May 1934. By then the company's trans-Tasman liner *Monowai* was seriously losing money, unable to compete with the big new US Matson luxury liners that were operating between Auckland and Sydney on the final leg of their trans-Pacific service. The *Monterey* and *Mariposa* were each capable of 22 knots and if the Union Company was to match them and regain its dominance on the Tasman Sea, it would have to come up with a ship of equal or greater speed that could get to Sydney from Auckland in two and a half days. The *Wanganella* by comparison took three and a half days at her speed of 14 knots.

The *Awatea* was conceived in response to this need. All design work was done at the Union Steam Ship Company's Head Office in Wellington, New Zealand and on 24th December 1934 the tender to build her that had been received from the Vickers-Armstrongs Ltd. shipyard at Barrow-in-Furness, England was accepted. First keel plates for Hull 707, as she was known during construction, were laid on 14th June 1935. Eight months later she was ready for launching. Elaine, Lady Bledisloe, wife of a former New Zealand Governor-General, named the new ship *Awatea* and sent her down the ways into Walney Channel at Barrow-in-Furness on the morning of Tuesday 25th February 1936.

Right: Grey murky weather and launch day at Vickers-Armstrongs Ltd. for Hull 707, 256 days after the laying of her first keel plates. The time is shortly after 11.00 on 25th February 1936. Having been named *Awatea* by her sponsor, she has just gone down the ways and dropped off the way-ends. Such are the stresses on a hull that this moment is said to be the most critical of a ship's structural life. The *Awatea* will be fully afloat for the very first time a few seconds after this photo was taken. [The Dock Museum, Barrow-in-Furness. Catalogue no V2410]

Below right: Both sets of the *Awatea's* propulsion turbines and their gear wheels in the turbine erecting shop at Vickers-Armstrongs. At left, one of the turbine sets has its outer casing in place while, at right, a turbine rotor with its many rings of stainless steel blades on their central drum is being moved by overhead crane. Once fully assembled, the turbine sets will be tested before they are lifted aboard the *Awatea*. Each of the two sets comprised three turbines, one set on each propeller shaft. High-pressure superheated steam from the boilers passed successively through three stages: a high-pressure impulse turbine, an intermediate-pressure reaction turbine and finally, largest of all, a low-pressure reaction turbine. The high-pressure turbines revolved at a maximum 2,363 rpm and the intermediate and low-pressure turbines at 1,690 rpm; the gear-wheels in turn reduced this to 125 rpm for the propeller shafts. [The Dock Museum, Barrow-in-Furness. Catalogue no 2826]

Awatea's engine starting platform, the very heart of the ship. It was from here that Henry Lockhart, the *Awatea's* Chief Engineer from 1936 to 1941, controlled and monitored the turbines along with his staff of engineers. The big brass wheels at right and left are the steam throttles, one for each set of turbines. An engine telegraph can be seen at left of centre. What a thrill it must have been to stand on the plates at right and listen to the rising howl of the turbines as the throttles were opened and the *Awatea* worked up to her top speed. On one trans-Pacific voyage in 1940 all six boilers were fired after a German surface raider alert, the *Awatea* reaching 26 knots. Henry Lockhart was succeeded as Chief Engineer by Harold Simmonds, who was awarded the Distinguished Service Cross (DSC) for his conduct during the time of the Awatea's loss. The *Awatea's* Chief Officer and Senior Third Officer received the same award. *[The Dock Museum, Barrow-in-Furness. Catalogue no Aw1-44]*

Inside the *Awatea's* engine room, showing steam lines and part of the tops of the turbine casings. Only on rare occasions were the turbines worked up to their maximum power with all six Yarrow oil-fired water-tube boilers making steam. Four boilers were sufficient to give the *Awatea* her 21-22 knot service speed. Usually a fifth boiler would be out of service for routine maintenance while a sixth could be lit if the ship was delayed by bad weather. Like all complex, very high performance machinery, the *Awatea's* turbines required careful, delicate handling. Running them at maximum power, with all boilers fired, involved the risk of excessive wear and tear with the ship potentially having to be taken out of service for lengthy repairs. *[The Dock Museum, Barrow-in-Furness. Catalogue no Aw1-43]*

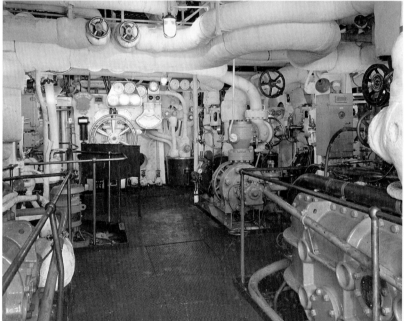

The emergency dynamo room and associated electrical switchboard at the aft end of the first class Sports Deck aboard the *Awatea*. This facility comprised a Petters diesel generator set producing 150 kW for essential services when the *Awatea's* main engines were shut down or should they become disabled. *[Wellington City Archives, New Zealand 2006 -15 -1-23 image 002]*

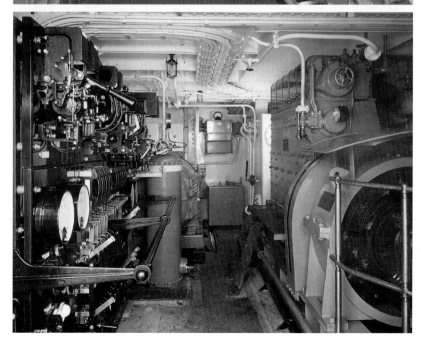

Fitting out of the ship now began, with the *Awatea* scheduled to be complete and ready for her acceptance trials by the end of July 1936. On the 22nd of that month she left Barrow for the Mersey, where she was placed in the graving dock at the Birkenhead shipyard of Cammell Laird to have her hull cleaned. The *Awatea* then left for the Firth of Clyde, where her acceptance trials were conducted. On 27th July, during these trials, the *Awatea* reached 22.5 knots with only four of her six boilers making steam. The following day she was handed over to the Union Steam Ship Company, Captain A.H. Davey formerly of the *Monowai* having been appointed her first master. She sailed from Greenock on her delivery voyage to New Zealand on 5th August 1936 and reached Wellington on the morning of Thursday 3rd September. Eleven days later the *Awatea* departed Auckland with passengers on her maiden Tasman crossing to Sydney.

She destroyed the competition with her destroyer-like speed. The *Awatea* running her acceptance trails in the Firth of Clyde in late July 1936, the house flag of her builders, Vickers-Armstrongs Ltd., at her mainmast. *[Above: Alexander Turnbull Library, Wellington New Zealand. War History Collection, F-36330-½, below: Ian J. Farquhar collection]*

The *Awatea* in the Mersey in late July 1936, just after she was completed. Leaving her fitting-out berth at Buccleuth Dock, Barrow-in-Furness, the *Awatea* made her very first sea voyage on 22nd July, steaming south to the Mersey. Here she was placed in the graving dock at Cammell Laird's Birkenhead shipyard for her hull to be cleaned of marine growth, prior to commencing her trials. Behind the *Awatea* is the famous waterfront of Liverpool.
[B. and A. Feilden/J. and M. Clarkson collection]

The *Awatea* was powered by two sets of Parsons single reduction geared turbines developing up to 23,881 shaft horse power, turning two propellers for a top speed that, with all six of her boilers making steam, exceeded 25 knots. Her power plant made the *Awatea* the third fastest merchant ship in the British Empire at the time of her construction. Electricity for the ship's hotel needs was delivered by three sets of turbo-generators each rated at 450 kW. There was also an emergency diesel generator able to produce 150kW of electricity.

Accommodation of the very highest standard was provided for 377 first class and 151 tourist class passengers. Facilities for the first class passengers rivalled the very best anywhere in the world at the time. Wide promenade decks and sumptuous public rooms extended the full length of the liner's centre superstructure, from below the bridge to the aft end of the boat deck. Second class passengers had more modest spaces at their disposal, these being located in the after part of the ship. There was also dormitory-type accomodation for 38 steerage passengers intended for groups of school children or migrant labourers. It comprised a tiny dining room above the propellers on C Deck together with fresh air next to the bollards and warping capstans on the *Awatea's* mooring deck right aft. Why such surroundings were deemed appropriate for children was a question that never had to be asked; union demands for additional crew numbers meant the steerage accommodation had to be converted into crew space while the ship was still fitting out.

The liner had a crew of 204, of whom 151 were cooks and stewards. Cargo space in four holds totalled 187,500 cubic feet, 23,500 of which was refrigerated. Mail was carried in the number one 'tween deck hold and number three hold was used for ship's stores and refrigerated cargo.

Under Captain Davey the *Awatea* gained a world-wide reputation for record-breaking passages across the Tasman and for arriving in port exactly on schedule. Captain Davey's talents were as much about publicity as they were seafaring; watched by crowds and cameras he would boldly manoeuvre the *Awatea* into and away from the wharves at Sydney, Wellington and Auckland entirely without the aid of tugs. His abilities in doing so were all the more remarkable given that, unlike modern ships, the 527-feet long *Awatea* had no side thrusters.

In the summer of 1937 the liner made her first and only cruise. She departed Auckland on the evening of Tuesday 19th January with all first and tourist cabins fully occupied. Over the course of three and a half days the cruise took the *Awatea* to Whangaroa, the Bay of Islands and Port Fitzroy on Great Barrier Island, all in northern New Zealand.

Annual refits for the Tasman liners were normally carried out during the mid-year winter

Left: Although undated, this photo was most probably taken just after the *Awatea* reached Wellington on 3rd September 1936, at the conclusion of her record-breaking delivery voyage from England which took her 28 days, 11 hours and 10 minutes. Lifted out of the water in Wellington's Jubilee Floating Dock on the afternoon of 5th September, the *Awatea's* bow displays the results of high-speed steaming with loss of paint right up to her anchor housing. Her underwater hull was repainted while she was in the dock, then on 15th September the *Awatea* departed for Auckland and her first Tasman crossing. The dock was the same one in which the *Wanganella* was repaired in 1947-48.
[Wellington City Archives, New Zealand 2006 -15 -1-20 image 001]

The *Awatea's* radio office. The ship's radio equipment was supplied by Amalgamated Wireless (Australasia) Ltd. and included a radio telephone. Passengers could use this facility to call any phone number in Australia and New Zealand while in mid-Tasman, an unheard-of novelty at the time. The *Awatea* had her own listed telephone number. During her first years, concerts by the *Awatea's* five-person orchestra were broadcast via the ship's radio transmitters to listeners in both Australia and New Zealand until the New Zealand Government, worried about competition against its own stations, put a stop to this. *[The Dock Museum, Barrow-in-Furness, England. Catalogue no Aw1-09]*

The main galley, which was located on B Deck between the first and tourist class dining rooms. At left, its switchboard and electrical cables overhead, is the main cooking range which had ten ovens, five per side. Food preparation equipment included potato peelers, a sausage machine, egg boilers, electric toasters and dough mixers one of which can be seen at right. All of it was supplied by the General Electric Co. Ltd. of London. Impeccable cuisine was part of the Tasman experience; Huddart Parker and the *Wanganella* were particularly famous for their dining room service. To this end the *Awatea* carried twenty one cooks, five bakers and six butchers. There were two sittings for lunch and dinner in each of the dining rooms. *[The Dock Museum, Barrow-in-Furness, England. Catalogue no Aw1-40]*

Inside the wheelhouse of the *Awatea,* looking through the open sliding door to the starboard bridge wing with part of the wing cab visible. The *Awatea's* navigating equipment included a Sperry gyro compass and automatic pilot, a British Admiralty-type recording echo sounder, Husun liquid magnetic compasses and a 30-day continuous course recorder. The bridge and wheelhouse were constructed in varnished teak. Aft of the wheelhouse was the chartroom, the open door to which can be seen just above and slightly to the left of the steering wheel. *[The Dock Museum, Barrow-in-Furness, England. Catalogue no Aw1-08]*

Above left: Looking aft from the roof of the starboard wing cab across the bridge island and Sports Deck of the *Awatea*. This deck, uppermost in the ship, featured three full-size tennis courts located between the *Awatea*'s funnels. The area at right, enclosed by the varnished timber bulwark, is just aft of the chart room. At lower left is the starboard accident boat, 22 feet in length and with seating for 33. All the *Awatea*'s lifeboats were made by Birmal Boats of Southampton using a corrosion-resistant alloy known as Birmabright. They were sent to Barrow-in-Furness aboard railway wagons. The ten larger lifeboats were 30 feet long, had an 80-person capacity, and were fitted with Fleming hand-propelling gear. *[The Dock Museum, Barrow-in-Furness. Catalogue no Aw1-03]*

Above right: Right forward in the ship, looking back at the *Awatea*'s foremast and bridge. In the centre of the picture is the electric windlass with its extended warping drums. Outboard of it, to port and starboard, are two electric warping capstans. It was use of this gear that enabled Captain A.H. Davey, the *Awatea*'s Master, to so expertly place his ship alongside the berth without the aid of tugs and then get her off the berth on sailing day also without tugs. *[The Dock Museum, Barrow-in-Furness. Catalogue no Aw1-04]*

Left: The *Awatea*'s first class promenade deck on the starboard side of the ship, looking aft. The two dark timber doors facing the camera in the middle of the picture led to a vestibule that, in turn, opened onto the first class lounge. Tall windows at right illuminated a long gallery running from the lounge to the music room at the forward end of the promenade deck. *[The Dock Museum, Barrow-in-Furness. Catalogue no Aw1-06]*

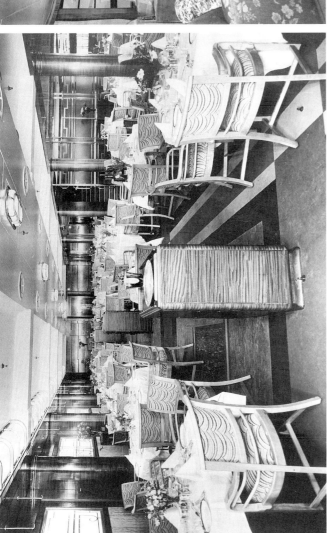

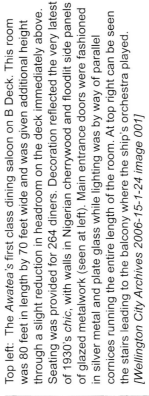

Top left: The *Awatea*'s first class dining saloon on B Deck. This room was 80 feet in length by 70 feet wide and was given additional height through a slight reduction in headroom on the deck immediately above. Seating was provided for 264 diners. Decoration reflected the very latest of 1930's *chic*, with walls in Nigerian cherrywood and floodlit side panels of glazed metalwork (seen at left). Main entrance doors were fashioned in silver metal and plate glass while lighting was by way of parallel cornices running the entire length of the room. At top right can be seen the stairs leading to the balcony where the ship's orchestra played. *[Wellington City Archives 2006-15-1-24 image 001]*

Top right: Forward on the *Awatea*'s promenade deck was the first class music room. Even in black and white the plushness of the furnishings in this room are fully apparent. At top left is the grand piano. Sycamore and walnut timber panelling adorns the walls, while the colour scheme for the chairs is recorded as having been blue with tables finished in pale gold. *[Wellington City Archives, New Zealand 2006-15-1-24 image 002]*

Left: Immediately aft of the music room was the first class library and writing room. Small in size, with six writing desks (three at left and three at right) the room was fitted with book cases at its forward end. In this photo the shelves have yet to be filled with the *Awatea*'s reading library. *[Wellington City Archives, New Zealand 2006-15-1-24 image 006]*

Right upper and lower: Amidships on the promenade deck was the *Awatea*'s magnificent first class lounge, the most elaborate room in the ship and among the finest ever to be seen on the Tasman Sea. Two decks high, it had a gallery along its upper sides and, in the top photo, a full-size cinema screen concealed behind sliding panels. The artwork featured on the panels was in gold and silver with a background of soft green. Tall windows gave views over the sea. The lower photo looks towards the forward port corner of the lounge and shows, at right, the black and gold marble surround in which a radiant electric fire was set. Above the fire, inside the marble surround, was a large mirror in tinted plate glass. [Wellington City Archives, New Zealand 2006 -15 -1-24 images 003 and 005]

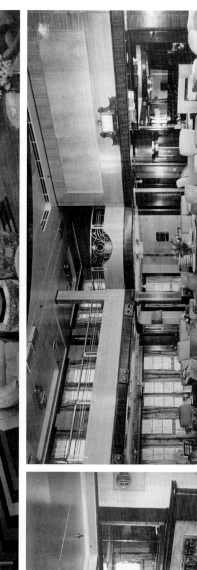

Below; The *Awatea*'s tourist class lounge on A Deck, aft in the ship. A much more modest room by comparison to the first class lounge, it offered tourist passengers just a taste of the luxury enjoyed by their social betters one deck above. The photo shows the entire room; forward of it was a smoke room of even smaller proportions. When the *Awatea* was fully booked with 151 tourist passengers, there must have been some competition of an evening for the not-too-many lounge chairs available in this room. [Wellington City Archives, New Zealand 2006 -15 -1-24 image 004]

Awatea dressed overall with flags, arriving at Sydney for the very first time on the morning of 18th September 1936. *[Wellington City Archives, New Zealand 2006 -15 -1-20 image 004]*

Another view, with the harbour bridge in the distance, of the *Awatea's* maiden arrival at Sydney. *[Wellington City Archives, New Zealand 2006 -15 -1-20 image 002]*

months, when passenger numbers were at their lowest. Although it was less than a year since her completion, problems had been experienced with the *Awatea's* turbine gearing. This needed to be rectified while still covered by the builder's warranty and ahead of the peak season at year's end. Between May and July 1937 the *Awatea* was withdrawn from service, her place being taken by the *Monowai*. As well as installation of new gear wheels, the *Awatea's* passenger accommodation was reconditioned and both her funnels were heightened by nine feet for more effective smoke dispersal. When engine trials were carried out off Sydney on 27th July, unconfirmed newspaper reports stated that the *Awatea* had reached speeds of over 26 knots. Resuming her Tasman schedule, the speed competition between the *Awatea* and the US liners now became headline news in both Australia and New Zealand. The *Monterey* held the record for the fastest Tasman crossing but when she arrived at Sydney Heads late on the evening of Monday 4th October 1937, the *Awatea* had broken the *Monterey's* record by two hours and 44 minutes. Her time of two days, seven hours and 28 minutes for the 1,281 mile journey, at an average speed of 23.1 knots, was not surpassed for another 24 years until June 1961 when the *Oriana* (41,915/1960) reached Sydney from Auckland in 47.5 hours at an average speed of 27 knots. The public acclaim was such that even the Prime Minister of Australia was among those who

offered his congratulations to the *Awatea* and Captain Davey. A stainless steel racing greyhound, five feet seven inches in length, was mounted at the truck of the liner's foremast to mark her achievement as the fastest ship on the Tasman Sea.

When the Second World War began in September 1939, the *Awatea* was undergoing her annual refit at Sydney. Keeping her peacetime colours she maintained the usual service on the Tasman until mid-1940, the only difference being the installation of a four-inch gun on the roof of the deckhouse at her stern. But following the loss of the Union Steam Ship Company's liner *Niagara* on 19th June 1940, it was decided to transfer the *Awatea* to the trans-Pacific service to take the *Niagara's* place. Next month Captain Davey left the *Awatea*, having asked to be relieved of command because of worsening arthritis in his legs. He was replaced by Captain W. Martin, the *Niagara's* Master.

Before commencing her first trans-Pacific sailing, the *Awatea* was sent to Manila to uplift 1,000 women and children evacuated from Hong Kong. She then departed Auckland for Vancouver on 10th September 1940 with 600 airmen from Australia and New Zealand aboard, bound for Canada under the Empire Air Training Scheme. The *Awatea* made two round trips to Vancouver then at the end of 1940 was diverted to Colombo with 700 troops, sailing in a convoy that included the *Queen Mary, Aquitania* and

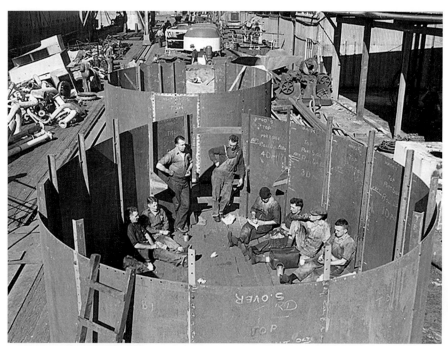 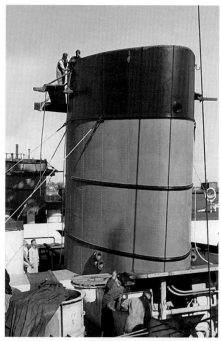

Between May and July 1937, seven and a half months following her entry into service, the *Awatea* underwent her first refit. New and improved turbine gearing was installed and both her funnels were heightened by nine feet to improve the discharge of soot and smuts from her boiler uptakes. Much of this waste had been falling on the liner's after decks, bringing complaints from passengers and necessitating much work keeping the decks clean. The refit was carried out at the Cockatoo Dockyard in Sydney, where dockyard workers pause in the assembly of the new funnel sections (above left). The man sitting at right, closest to the opening in the funnel plates, is probably studying the form for that afternoon's gallops at Randwick Race Course. The leather satchel beside his companion at right was an accessory carried by all Sydney waterfront workers at the time. Repainting of the after funnel (above right) is near complete after the fitting of its new section. The forward funnel awaits rebuilding. It was reported that when the *Awatea* ran full power trials off Sydney on 27th July 1937 at the conclusion of her refit, she attained a top speed of 26.35 knots. *[Ian J. Farquhar collection]*

The raising of the *Awatea's* funnels in mid-1937 gave her a bigger, more powerful look. She is seen here in Sydney Harbour. Compare her new profile to the views of her on her trials just after the ship was built. The second funnel, which is not emitting smoke, was a dummy. *[Wellington City Archives, New Zealand 2006 -15 -1-21 image 001]*

Dominion Monarch. Two further trips to Vancouver followed and it was there at the beginning of September 1941 that the *Awatea* was requisitioned for war service by the British Ministry of War Transport.

Ordered to proceed to Britain for conversion to a troop ship, and painted entirely in grey, the *Awatea* departed Vancouver on Thursday 11th September 1941. Early the following morning, having encountered fog, she was rammed by the American tanker *M.E. Lombardi* while in Spanish Roads off

Victoria at the southern end of Vancouver Island. The liner put back to Vancouver for repairs, and while there the work of converting her to a troop ship with improved anti-aircraft armament was also done. In her new capacity the *Awatea* made a number of trooping voyages in convoy and it was on one of these while in fog on the night of 22nd August 1942 that she rammed the destroyer USS *Buck* (1,570d/1939) off the Newfoundland Banks. A depth charge went overboard from the destroyer as a result of the impact

Leaving Vancouver during the early war period when she was employed on the trans-Pacific route, the *Awatea* is seen here steaming under the Lions Gate Bridge. *[V H. Young and L.A. Sawyer]*

Only the gun at her stern and numerous promenade deck windows painted out give an indication that life is anything other than normal for the *Awatea* in this photo. Her brief reign on the Tasman Sea has, however, already come to its end. Here she is at Brisbane on 13th August 1940, most probably while on her way to Manila in the Philippines to embark 1,000 evacuees from Hong Kong. The stainless steel racing greyhound attesting to her record-breaking speed is visible at the top of the liner's foremast. *[V.H. Young and L.A. Sawyer]*

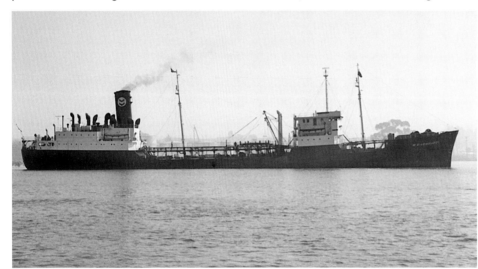

A post-war view of the US tanker *M.E. Lombardi* taken many years after she rammed the *Awatea* in the Strait of Juan de Fuca off Vancouver Island on the night of 11-12 September 1941. Owned by the Standard Oil Company of California, the 5,325 grt *M.E. Lombardi* was completed in 1940 by the Sun Shipbuilding and Dry Dock Company of Chester, Pennsylvania. In 1972 she was sold to Nasugbu Navigation Company of Manila, and was renamed *Nasugbu*. Under this name she was broken up in the Philippines four years later. *[V.H. Young and L.A. Sawyer]*

The *Awatea's* war service did not begin well. Having been transferred to the Canadian Australasian Line's trans-Pacific service to replace the lost *Niagara*, the liner had arrived at Vancouver in early September 1941 at the end of what was her last commercial voyage. While there the *Awatea* was requisitioned for use as a troopship and ordered to proceed to Britain for conversion to her new role. She left Vancouver on 11th September with her hull, funnels and superstructure painted wartime grey, but she had only been at sea for six hours when, early the following morning, she collided in fog with the small U.S. tanker *M.E. Lombardi*. The *Awatea* returned immediately to Vancouver where these photos were taken. They show the considerable damage done to the *Awatea's* port side hull and the scale of repairs that were needed. While these were underway the liner's interior was converted for troop carrying, and she duly left Vancouver on 27th October 1941 with 2,000 Canadian infantry reinforcements for the British garrison at Hong Kong. *[North Vancouver Museum and Archives, 27-2828 and 27-2831]*

and exploded beneath the *Awatea*, lifting her out of the sea. She was repaired at Halifax before proceeding to Glasgow where in October 1942 the *Awatea* was converted to an infantry landing ship for use in the Allied landings in North Africa.

Known as Operation Torch, the landings comprised three large convoys of troops with the *Awatea* in the convoy destined for Algiers. Here on the night of 8-9th November 1942 her troops went ashore in the ship's landing barges. Later that day the *Awatea* was detailed to take the place of the troop ship *Strathnaver* (22,547/1931) which was disabled with boiler problems, in a further landing operation. Ammunition and petrol for RAF Spitfires was loaded on 10th November and at 11.10 pm the *Awatea* departed Algiers for the Bay of Bougie, 120 miles to the east, with the destroyers HMS *Bicester* and HMS *Wilton* (both 1,050/1941) as escort. Arriving early next morning, 11th November, her cargo was successfully landed despite constant enemy air attacks and then at 4 pm the *Awatea* got underway with her escort, having been ordered to return to Algiers and then Gibraltar. Unfortunately, some of the petrol and ammunition was still onboard. At 4.10 pm when only a mile out to sea, the *Awatea* was caught by a formation of six Savoia-Marchetti SM.79 *Sparviero* torpedo bombers. Earlier sorties by the Italian Regia Aeronautica that day had been repulsed by fierce AA gun barrages from the many Allied ships lying in the Bay of Bougie. The *Awatea* had still to work up to the 26 knots that might have saved her. Singling her out and delivering their attacks with precision, the SM.79s quickly made two direct hits forward in the ship.

One bomb went into the number two hold, the explosion catapulting the steel hatch cover up over the bridge and funnels. Ammunition in the hold detonated, the blast setting the fore part of the *Awatea* alight. Captain G.B. Morgan DSC of the Union Steam Ship Company, who had taken command of the *Awatea* on 25th March 1942, turned back towards the land intending to beach her, but an Italian aircraft next put an aerial torpedo into the *Awatea's* port side, flooding the engine room. Two further bombs hit the ship. HMS *Bicester* and the Flower class corvette HMS *Pentstemon* (925/1941) both came alongside to try and douse the fires. With *Awatea* dead in the water, burning furiously, listing to 40 degrees and with her turbines stilled, Captain Morgan had no choice but to order fire-fighting efforts halted and the *Awatea* abandoned. The last that was seen of her was the ship lit up by flames in the night, the New Zealand Ensign still flying from the gaff at the *Awatea's* mainmast.

Remarkably there were just four wounded and no fatalities. The *Awatea's* gunners shot down two of the attacking aircraft and claimed three others damaged. Taken to Liverpool aboard the Dutch *Marnix van St. Aldegonde* (19,355/1930), her crew were back in New Zealand by March 1943. For his outstanding leadership Captain George Brotherton Morgan was awarded the Distinguished Service Order and Lloyd's War Medal for Bravery at Sea. Sixteen members of the *Awatea's* crew were also recognised.

The *Awatea* was the only international merchant ship manned by a New Zealand crew to take part in combat operations during the Second World War. Today her remains lie in deep water off Cap Carbon in Algeria, North Africa, far from the Tasman Sea and the shores of New Zealand. Heroic in peace and war, *Awatea* shall always rank as that country's greatest-ever passenger liner.

Farewell to the *Awatea*: bombed, set on fire and sunk just three days after this photo was taken. She is at left, bow to the camera, lying at anchor off Algiers B Beachhead during the November 1942 Operation Torch landings in North Africa. The warship passing in front of her is the Hunt class Type II escort destroyer HMS *Wilton* (1,050/1941).

All the ships behind the *Awatea* were, like her, passenger liners converted into infantry landing ships. At left, partially obscured by the *Awatea*, is the Orient Line's *Otranto* (20,032/1926). The infantry landing ship HMS *Keren* (12,150/1930) is directly astern of the *Awatea*. Behind HMS *Keren* is Union-Castle's *Winchester Castle*

(20,109/1930). In the background at far right is the Australian liner *Bulolo* (6,267/1938). She had been converted in June 1942 to become the Royal Navy's first Landing Ship Headquarters. The *Awatea* was much faster than any of these ships but, unlike her, they all survived the war. (*IWM A12727*)

General arrangement drawings of *Awatea*

Vickers-Armstrongs and the Union Steamship Company were justifiably proud of their new building and gave the proprietors of the weekly shipping magazine 'Shipbuilding and Shipping Record' the facilities they needed to describe and illustrate the ship. By 1935 reproduction of material in technical journals was reaching a high standard and general arrangement drawings like this were becoming more common and more detailed. [*Andrew Bell collection*]

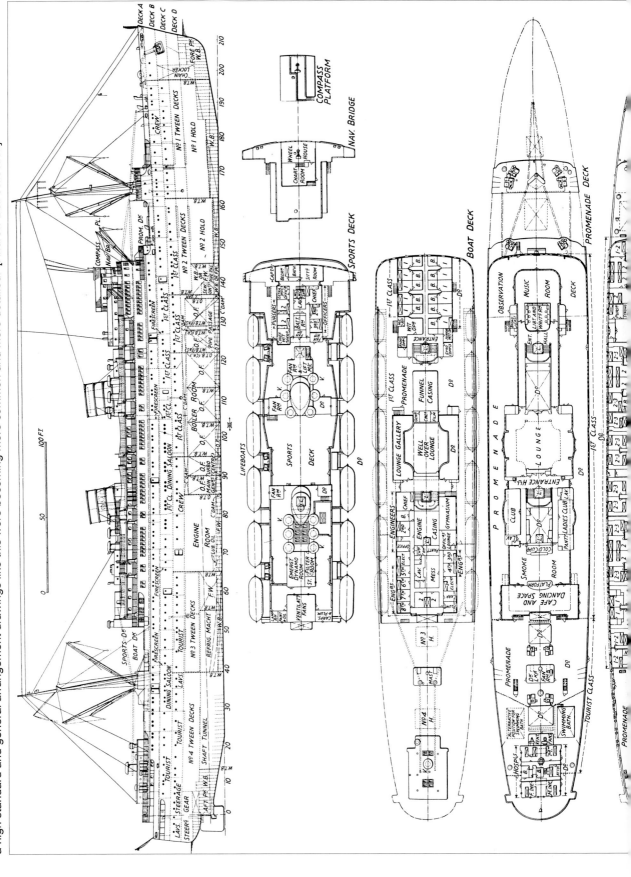

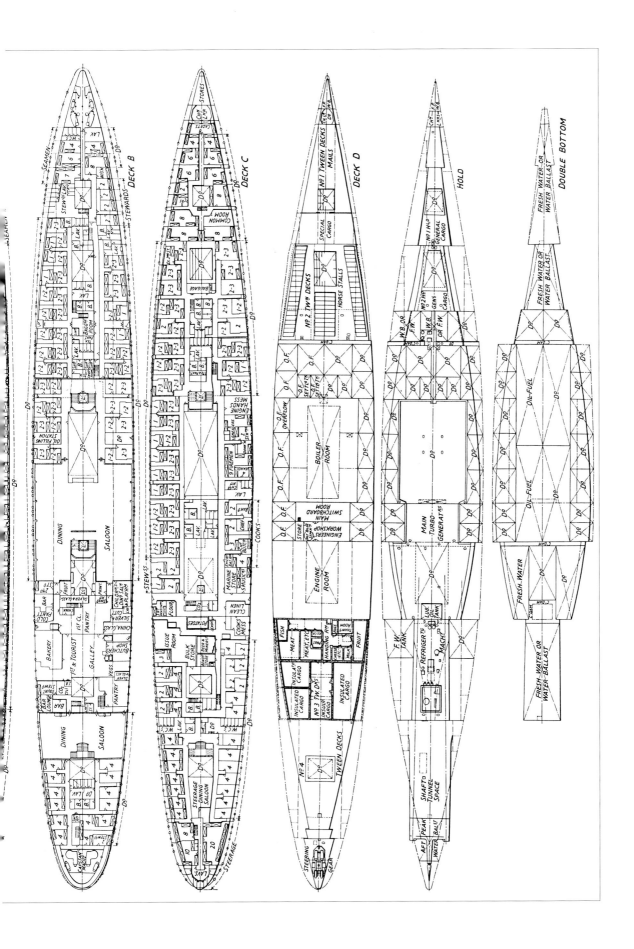

73

The *Monowai* as she was before the Second World War, going astern from Queens Wharf in Wellington on a 1930s winter's day at the commencement of a trans-Tasman voyage. This photo shows to good effect the high and very impressive bridge she carried in those times. The varnished teak bridge with which she was fitted during her post-war refit, though handsome, was not quite as imposing. *[Alexander Turnbull Library, Wellington, New Zealand. Photographer: E T Robson. C-22391-½]*

MONOWAI - GRAND OLD LADY OF THE TASMAN

Razmak

Like the *Wanganella*, the *Monowai* became an institution in the ports of Sydney, Auckland and Wellington during the 1950s. Having spent the last of the pre-war years either laid up or utilised only for relieving other passenger liners, she came into her own from 1949 when 24 years old, an age when most of her contemporaries were reaching the end of their economic lives.

The *Monowai* was built for P&O as *Razmak* to replace the *Salsette* (5,842/1908). Torpedoed in July 1917, this liner had run her owner's fortnightly express passenger and mail service between Bombay and Aden, her 20-knot speed making her the fastest ship in P&O's fleet. A replacement for the lost *Salsette* emerged from Harland and Wolff in 1925 in the form of a vessel with similar layout. Built at Greenock, where her keel was laid on 20th June 1923, yard number 659 was launched by Viscountess Inchcape, wife of P&O's Chairman, on Thursday 16th October 1924 and given the name *Rasmak*, although this was subsequently amended to *Razmak*. Her two quadruple-expansion four-cylinder steam

engines were manufactured by Harland and Wolff at Belfast and it was to there that she was towed immediately after launch. Boilers and engines were placed aboard and all fitting out was done at Belfast. She was ready for sea on 26th February 1925 when hand-over to her owners took place. The *Razmak* proceeded to London then departed on Friday 13th March 1925 for her maiden voyage to Aden.

At 10,602 gross register tonnage and 519 feet in length overall, the *Razmak* had accommodation for 142 first class passengers and 142 in second class plus 108 in steerage. Twelve hydraulic cranes served six holds having 131,460 cubic feet of cargo space. She was a very good-looking ship with her slim raked funnels, two masts, vertical stem and elegant counter stern. The two sets of quadruple-expansion engines, each turning one of two propellers, developed 12,000 indicated horse power giving a maximum speed of 18 knots, not quite as fast as her predecessor. There were six boilers four of which were double-ended and two single-ended, burning oil under forced draught to supply steam at 215 psi.

Hull number 659 ready for launch day with all staging dismantled, leaving only the timber uprights. The launch platform is waiting in front of her bow for the naming ceremony. *[Ulster Folk and Transport Museum, 1848]*

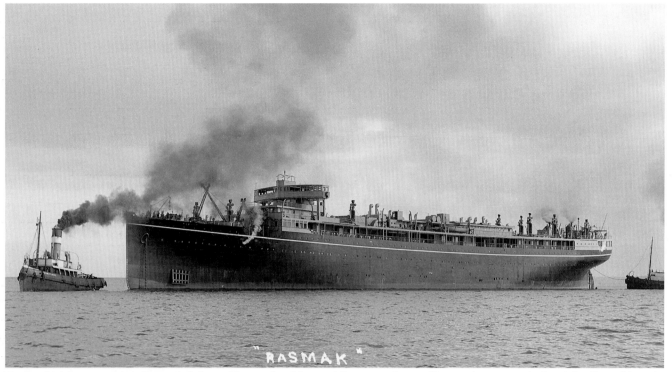

Having just been named *Rasmak* (later changed to *Razmak)* by her sponsor, Viscountess Inchcape, the ship is afloat for the first time following her launch. Remnants of the port fore-poppet are still attached to her bow. Fitting out was done at Harland and Wolff's Belfast yard but it is interesting to note the gear already in place on her upper decks at the time of launch. This includes all the hydraulic cargo cranes and at least one lifeboat. *[B. and A. Feilden/J. and M. Clarkson collection]*

The new ship had hardly settled into her Bombay-Aden routine when, in 1926, the service was discontinued by P&O. The need for a feeder ship between these two ports was removed following the introduction of P&O's *Cathay* (15,104/1925), *Comorin* (15,116/1925) and *Chitral* (15,248/1925) for their Australian mail and passenger service. It was found that these liners could include a call at Bombay as well as Aden while still maintaining their schedules. Designed specifically for the Aden-Bombay run and too small for use on other P&O routes, a new 12-day service linking Marseilles and Bombay was put in place for the *Razmak*. It was not a success and, in the deepening trade recession following the 1929 Wall Street crash, there seemed no future for the near-new liner. In July 1930 she returned to England and was laid up at Tilbury.

Transfer to Union Steam Ship

Salvation came with the death of another ship on the other side of the world. On 17th August 1930 the Union Steam Ship Company of New Zealand's veteran *Tahiti* (7,585/1904, formerly *Port Kingston*) foundered in mid-Pacific while bound from Wellington to San Francisco via Rarotonga and Tahiti with 103 passengers and 149 crew. The liner's starboard propeller shaft had broken off two days earlier, tearing a large hole in her side. All passengers and crew along with mails and a shipment of bullion were saved. With the loss of the *Tahiti* the Union Steam Ship Company was, like Huddart Parker a few years later, suddenly in need of a new liner. The *Razmak* was judged to be ideal for its trans-Pacific route and was duly transferred within the P&O Group to the Union

The *Razmak* fully complete and in the graving dock beside Harland and Wolff's fitting-out jetties in Abercorn Basin, Queen's Island, Belfast. Her hull is being painted in readiness for the liner's delivery to her owners. *[Ulster Folk and Transport Museum, 1941]*

The beginning of a 35 year life at sea that, unknown to her owners when this photo was taken, would confer great success and affection on the *Razmak* but only after she had sailed to another part of the world and been given an entirely different name. Here the *Razmak* displays the sombre livery worn by liners of the Peninsula and Oriental Steam Navigation Company before the Second World War: black hull and funnels; brownstone coloured superstructure. With her twin masts and funnels, all well-raked, she was a most handsome ship. *[Ulster Folk and Transport Museum, 1957]*

This grand old steam ship with her lofty funnel, open bridge and finely raked masts is the Union Steam Ship Company's 7,585 gross register tonnage *Tahiti*. Built on the Clyde in 1904 as the *Port Kingston* for the Imperial Direct West India Mail Company, she was purchased in August 1911 for the Union Company's trans-Pacific service to San Francisco. Her new owners found her to be an excellent ship that for the next two decades gave them every satisfaction. The only blemish came on 3rd November 1927 when the *Tahiti* rammed and sank the Sydney Harbour ferry *Greycliffe* with the deaths of 42 people.

The *Tahiti* does not enter our story until the very end of her life. She foundered in mid-Pacific on passage to San Francisco via Rarotonga, when her starboard propeller shaft broke early on the morning of Friday 15th August 1930. Before it could be stopped the still-revolving shaft opened bulkheads and tore a large hole in the liner's side. Her engineers and seamen kept the *Tahiti* afloat for two days until all passengers and crew, mail, gold bullion and baggage were transferred to rescue vessels. The *Tahiti's* loss meant the Union Company had sudden need for a replacement liner, and the choice fell upon the unwanted *Razmak*. At the time of her sinking the *Tahiti's* Master was Captain A.T. Toten, who went on to be appointed the *Monowai's* first Master. *[Ian J. Farquhar collection]*

The *Monowai* arriving at Wellington for the first time in November 1930, direct from London, after she had been acquired by the Union Steam Ship Company. The liner is still in P&O colours with the P&O house flag at her bow. She is completing a turn to starboard in the inner harbour, with Oriental Bay and Mount Victoria behind her, preparatory to coming alongside Queens Wharf. *[Alexander Turnbull Library, Wellington, New Zealand. F-135949-½]*

A stern view of the *Monowai* berthed at Queens Wharf in Wellington, New Zealand shortly after she had been repainted in the colours of the Union Steam Ship Company. *[V.H. Young and L.A. Sawyer]*

Company in September 1930. She was renamed *Monowai*, the company's second ship to bear this name which means 'one water' in the Maori language. Passenger accommodation was altered to 280 first class and 203 second, and Bauer-Wach low-pressure double-reduction exhaust turbines were fitted to each of her reciprocating engines. Total output was now 14,740 indicated horse power, giving a maximum speed 19 knots. Still in her P&O colours, the *Monowai* departed London on 3rd October 1930 for Wellington, New Zealand. Here she was repainted in Union Company livery. Captain A.T. Toten, Master of the lost *Tahiti*, was given command and on 2nd December 1930 the *Monowai* began her inaugural trans-Pacific voyage to San Francisco via Rarotonga, Pago Pago, Tahiti and Honolulu. One hundred and seventy five officers and crew were aboard.

This service averaged five round trips per year but, with the contraction in trade resulting from the Great Depression, the *Monowai* was soon found to be too big for the San Francisco route. She was instead employed on the Sydney-Vancouver run and then on the Union Company's trans-Tasman service before going back to San Francisco. On 19th May 1931 the *Monowai* made her first call at Auckland, berthing at Princess Wharf. Her Master by now was Captain T.B. Sewell. Then on 26th October 1932 the *Monowai* left San Francisco for the final time, the Union Company

having decided to use her permanently on the Tasman Sea between Sydney, Auckland, Melbourne and Wellington. Here she would be up against the newer but slower *Wanganella* and the much more prestigious *Mariposa* (18,017/1931) and *Monterey* (18,017/1932), just introduced by the the USA's Matson Line. The *Monowai's* port of registry was changed from London to Wellington. On 24th November 1932 at Sydney, Captain A.H. Davey took command of the ship. One of the Union Company's most successful and best-remembered masters, Arthur Davey (1878-1966) remained in command until early June 1936 when he was sent to England to take charge of the new *Awatea*.

During Captain Davey's tenure the *Monowai* gained a reputation as a fast ship, making a number of swift passages from Sydney to Wellington the best of which, in May 1934, took her just 63 hours and 10 minutes at an average speed of 19.8 knots. Over the summer period of December to March each year she made what must have been delightful cruises to Fiordland in southern New Zealand, throughout the Marlborough Sounds at the top of the Sound Island, and to the Hauraki Gulf and Bay of Islands north of Auckland. On 9th January 1934 the *Monowai* visited Port Chalmers (Otago, New Zealand) for the first time, where she berthed at the George Street Wharf. The previous month she had suffered minor damage off Sydney during particularly heavy weather. In February

This is the Oceanic Steamship Company's *Monterey*. She is underway in Sydney Harbour, sailing past Rose Bay. Looking at her, it is clear the directors of both Huddart Parker and the Union Steam Ship Company had extremely good reason to be worried when they learned that this luxury liner and her sister the *Mariposa* were under construction and, once in service, would be carrying passengers across the Tasman. Both ships were big - just over

18,000 gross register tonnage, fast at 22 knots and with their stunning white-hulled looks the very epitome of 1930s glamour. Neither the *Wanganella* nor the *Monowai* were in their class but the Union Company's *Awatea* certainly was.

The *Monterey* was built by the Bethlehem Shipyard at Quincy, Massachusetts at a then-staggering cost of US$8,300,492, much of it sourced from a US Government loan (the letter

'M' for Matson - the Oceanic Steamship Company was a subsidiary of the Matson Line - was added to her funnels when these loans were eventually paid off). She was launched on 10th October 1931. Note the four large balconies just below the forward lifeboat. These were the *Monterey's* Lanai suites, four on each side of the ship and forerunners of today's cruise liners with their tiered decks of private balconies. *[Ian J. Farquhar collection]*

The prevailing wind in Wellington is the north-westerly, and in this wonderful shot taken on 10th February 1933 the gale is beam-on to the *Monowai* as she manoeuvres in the harbour. The liner is probably about to come alongside at the conclusion of a 'Sounds Cruise', hence the flags at her masts. *[Museum of Wellington Collection, New Zealand, Neg no 242]*

The wind-scarred hills of Pencarrow behind her, the *Monowai* in this photo taken on 10th May 1934 is steaming into a southerly gale as she heads out through the entrance to Wellington Harbour. The winds and seas in the entrance channel are but a foretaste of what lies ahead for those of a more delicate constitution among the *Monowai's* passengers. Soon, having cleared the harbour entrance, she will turn west into the Tasman Sea where sea conditions will likely be many times more boisterous. *[Museum of Wellington Collection, New Zealand, Neg no 243]*

Inside Milford Sound during one of the *Monowai's* Sounds Cruises to Fiordland, New Zealand in February 1933. Snow-capped mountains of the Southern Alps lie ahead of the ship. Boats are being lowered and the main accommodation ladder is rigged, ready to embark passengers for going ashore at the head of the Sound. *[Alexander Turnbull Library, Wellington, New Zealand. F-18737-½]*

A wonderful photo from the 1930s taken from right forward on the *Monowai's* forecastle, looking back towards her foremast and bridge framed by two of the liner's hydraulic cargo cranes. She is steaming up Milford Sound in the morning sun, with the towering, glacier-cut sides of the fiord on either side of her. Passengers crowd every vantage point to take in the majestic scenery. *[Alexander Turnbull Library, Wellington, New Zealand. G-75140-½]*

The *Monowai* as she was during the 1930s. The flag at the truck of her mainmast is that of the Canadian Australasian Line. This was a joint venture formed in July 1931 between the Union Steam Ship Company and Canadian Pacific to operate the trans-Pacific route from Sydney and Auckland to Vancouver. Incorporated in Canada, the Canadian Australasian Line was half-owned by the Union Company and by Canadian Pacific, and the Union Company's *Aorangi* and *Niagara* were transferred to it. When engaged on the Vancouver route as a relief ship, as in this photo, the *Monowai* flew the Canadian Australasian Line's flag. The line went out of existence in 1953 when the 29-year-old *Aorangi* was withdrawn and scrapped. The *Niagara* had been mined and lost in 1940 and was not replaced. *[V.H. Young and L.A. Sawyer]*

1935 Melbourne was dropped from the liner's regular itinerary and on the 13th of that month she cleared Port Phillip Bay for the final time.

In July 1935 the *Monowai* undertook a two-week South Sea Island winter cruise, visiting Tonga, Pago Pago in Samoa, and Fiji. More damage was caused to the *Monowai* during a very rough crossing in May 1936, passengers being confined to their cabins for the entire voyage. In January that year she diverted to Lord Howe Island in mid-Tasman in response to a call for medical assistance. In very bad weather two doctors and a nurse were landed from the ship to attend a seriously ill local resident. Having decided she must be evacuated, Captain Davey and the *Monowai's* Chief Officer, L.G. Ramsay, succeeded in getting the patient and her family aboard the *Monowai* despite horrendous sea conditions. In April 1934 the *Monowai* had performed a similar medical errand, going to the aid of the Finnish sail training ship *Favell*. A ship's cadet with acute appendicitis was taken off and brought to hospital in Wellington.

From mid-1936 the *Monowai* was laid up at Hobson Bay in Auckland, her place on the Tasman crossing having been taken by the *Awatea*. She remained in lay-up for nearly a year, then was temporarily put back into service to replace the Union Company's liner *Aorangi* (17,491/1924) on the trans-Pacific service to Vancouver while the *Aorangi* was under repair having damaged a crankshaft. Reconditioning, docking and painting the *Monowai* after her long lay-up took six weeks. On 3rd June 1937 she departed Auckland for

Captain Arthur Davey in 1935 when he was in command of the *Monowai*, just before he was appointed Master of the *Awatea*. A tough and hard-driving seafarer, renowned for his exceptional ship handling skills, he was also a very genial host to passengers aboard his ships. Born in Dunedin, New Zealand on 9th June 1878, the son of Welsh immigrant parents, Captain Davey joined the Union Steam Ship Company in January 1904. His first command, gained in August 1911, was the Union Company's collier *Kini* (1,122/1894). Captain Davey is best remembered for the four years he served as Master of the liner *Awatea*. Retiring from the Union Company in February 1941 because of poor health, Captain Davey lived in Auckland, New Zealand until his death on 1st March 1966, aged 85. *[Wellington City Archives, New Zealand Ref: AF005:11:14]*

Left: The cabin class lounge aboard the *Monowai*, as it was during her pre-war years. The photo looks across a modestly furnished and not overly large room, towards the base of the mainmast with its aft rake. The backs of the wooden chairs have a P&O monogram engraved into them. Note the parquet floor and buttons within easy reach on the wall panels for summoning stewards. *[Wellington City Archives, New Zealand. 2006/15:5:195]*

Below: Inside a deluxe first class cabin. There is an adjoining single cabin at left, through the open doorway. Air vents protrude from the deckhead above the white chair facing the camera, and also in the smaller cabin. This accommodation may have been retained for use by one of the *Monowai's* senior officers or her commanding officer when the ship was converted into an armed merchant cruiser at the Devonport Naval Dockyard in Auckland, though presumably the timber paneling would have been stripped out because of the fire hazard. *[Wellington City Archives, New Zealand. 2006/15:5:195]*

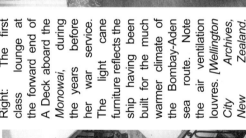

Below: A pre-1939 view of the *Monowai's* first class entrance on B Deck, forward in the ship. The two flights of stairs at right lead down to the first class dining saloon and the wide stairs between them go up to the first class lounge. The purser's bureau is at left while the narrow passageways in the centre of the picture, beyond the stairwell, lead to first class cabins. *[Wellington City Archives, New Zealand. 2006/15:5:195]*

Right: The first class lounge at the forward end of A Deck aboard the *Monowai*, during the years before her war service. The light cane furniture reflects the ship having been built for the much warmer climate of the Bombay-Aden sea route. Note the air ventilation louvres. *[Wellington City Archives, New Zealand. 2006/15:5:195]*

The *Monowai*'s first class dining room on C Deck (above), as it looked during the 1950s after having been refurbished following the liner's war service. The camera is pointing aft from the forward edge of the room. The captain's table with seating for eight is in the left foreground. *[Auckland Maritime Society Collection/New Zealand National Maritime Museum]*

The newly decorated first class lounge (top right), so well-known to passengers travelling aboard the *Monowai* in the 1950s. The panelled timber and glass barrier at right surrounds the stairs leading down to the first class entrance on B Deck. Doors at the forward end of the lounge, on either side of the book cases, lead to first class cabins right at the front of the *Monowai*'s superstructure, and also to the cinema projection room. Some of the chair upholstery appears not to be in best condition; note the fabric hanging down from the side of the timber-backed chair at mid-left, also the tatty fabric on the chair across the walkway to the right. There is a piano on the starboard side of the room (at far right) while outside the curtained windows is the first class promenade. *[Auckland Maritime Society Collection/New Zealand National Maritime Museum]*

The first class smoke room on A Deck (bottom right), at the aft end of the first class promenade. Judging by its older-style furnishings and panelling, this room was not given the full modernisation that the first class lounge and dining room received during the *Monowai*'s post-war rebuilding. At left is the bar, while at right is a narrow stairway down which gentlemen could make their way discreetly to their cabins on the deck below, perhaps after a few too many night-time whiskeys. *[Auckland Maritime Society Collection/New Zealand National Maritime Museum]*

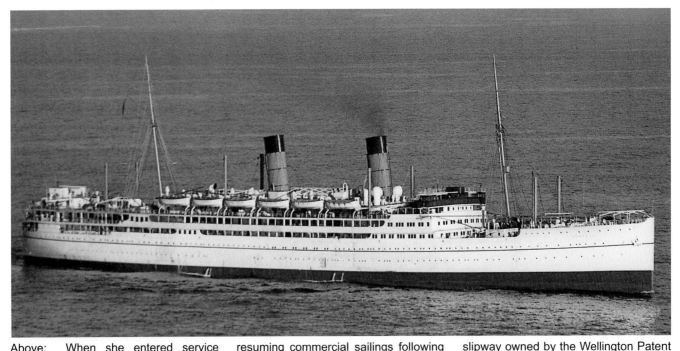

Above: When she entered service in January 1925 the *Aorangi* was the world's largest and fastest motor ship, and at 17,491 gross register tonnage she was also the largest passenger liner ever to be owned by the Union Steam Ship Company. Her Sulzer diesels drove four propellers for a top speed of 18 knots. This photo shows the majestic *Aorangi* as she was in 1948, immediately after resuming commercial sailings following war service. For her first two round voyages across the Pacific the *Aorangi* was given a white hull before reverting back to the Union Company's green livery. *[Ian J. Farquhar collection]*

Below: In 1911 the Union Steam Ship Company built a slipway and a large engineering workshop at Evans Bay in Wellington, beside an existing slipway owned by the Wellington Patent Slip Company (of which the Union Company was majority shareholder). Repair wharves were also built, along with a ships' stores warehouse and an extensive steam laundry. In this photo the *Monowai* is alongside at Evans Bay in 1939. Following the introduction of the *Awatea*, the *Monowai* was needed only for cruises and for temporarily replacing the Union Company's liners on either the trans-Pacific or the trans-Tasman services when these ships were withdrawn for annual refits. Here the *Monowai* is most probably being de-stored in readiness for lay-up. She was then moored off Kaiwharawhara on the western side of Wellington harbour, in an area known at the time as 'rotten row'. It was here that, during and after the Great Depression, the Union Company and other ship owners laid up their unwanted vessels. The twin funnelled ship behind the *Monowai* is most likely the Union Company's *Maori* (3,399/1907). *[John Marsh collection]*

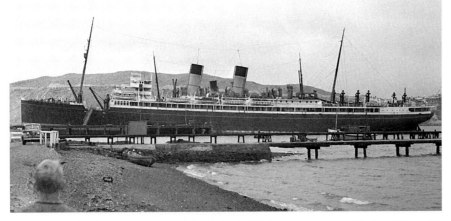

Sydney under the command of Captain A.T. Toten, the *Monowai's* first Master, with passengers, mail and general cargo, bound for Sydney. She was back in Auckland on 14th June then sailed the next day for Vancouver, arriving there on 4th July.

HMNZS *Monowai*

Apart from summer cruises and acting as a relief ship for the *Awatea* and the *Aorangi*, the *Monowai* now had little to do, spending considerable periods laid up until the Second World War intervened in 1939. At the time of her building, provision had been made for the *Monowai* to be converted to an armed merchant cruiser with decks strengthened for mounting eight six-inch guns. Laid up off Kaiwharawhara in Wellington from 2nd September 1939, the *Monowai* was taken on charter by the New Zealand Naval Board on 21st October and sent that same day to Devonport Naval Dockyard in Auckland. The Union Company was paid £5,000 per month by the New Zealand Government for use of the ship. Her eight guns were waiting for her in Auckland, having been shipped to New Zealand when she was transferred to Union Company ownership in 1930. During her conversion, which took ten months, all but two of the *Monowai's* big hydraulic cargo cranes were removed. It was hoped that the two left aboard might delude a less cautious enemy vessel into thinking she was a harmless merchantman.

HMNZS *Monowai*, pennant number F39, was commissioned as an armed merchant cruiser on 30th August 1940 under the command of Acting Captain H.P.V. McClintock RN, with a total complement of 366 officers and other ranks. Most

During her time as an armed merchant cruiser the *Monowai* provided an invaluable contribution to the New Zealand war effort, training hundreds of young men in the arts of seamanship, naval gunnery and marine engineering. Fortunately for them, her fighting qualities were never tested in combat against an enemy warship. She makes a brave sight, seen in Wellington Harbour in this photo, but HMNZS *Monowai's* superannuated guns and lack of high speed would not have given any commanding officer of the Kriegsmarine or the Imperial Japanese Navy reason for consternation had they come across her at sea. On the one occasion when the *Monowai* did encounter an enemy vessel, in the form of the Japanese submarine *I-20*, the action was cut short when the submarine crash dived and was not seen again. *[Alexander Turnbull Library, Wellington New Zealand, PICT-000170]*

of these were drawn from the Royal Naval Volunteer Reserve (New Zealand). The *Monowai's* engineer officers, needed because of their familiarity with her reciprocating machinery, were all given naval reserve rank. Extensive work had been required on the liner's boilers and engines to ensure they could deliver her full 19 knots.

HMNZS *Monowai's* armament consisted of eight single six-inch guns, four per side and all of pre-First World War vintage. Two three-inch AA guns were fitted along with a number of smaller AA weapons, and she also carried eight depth charges. Following commissioning, the ship spent seven weeks on trials and working up in the Hauraki Gulf area before sailing for Wellington on 21st October 1940. She arrived early on the morning of 23rd October and berthed alongside King's Wharf. Two days later New Zealand's War Cabinet came aboard to inspect the ship. On the morning of Sunday 27th October Prime Minister Peter Fraser paid a brief visit. Twenty New Zealand Army officers and two companies of 160 Infantry were embarked late that morning, then just after 12 noon it was the turn of the New Zealand Governor-General, Viscount Galway, to be received aboard. Watched by hundreds of

spectators HMNZS *Monowai* got under way on the afternoon of the same day, 27th October 1940, to begin her first wartime mission. This was escorting the Union Company's *Rangatira* (6,152/1931) with a contingent of troops bound for Suva, Fiji. She was back in Auckland on 6th November 1940.

Life as an armed merchant cruiser followed a similar pattern for the next 29 months: escort and patrol work around the New Zealand coast and the South Pacific islands. In that early phase of the war HMNZS *Monowai* with her ancient guns was the closest New Zealand had to a large warship stationed in home waters. On 30th December 1941 a shell exploded in the port six-inch gun located on the forecastle during gunnery exercises off Tiritirimatangi Island north of Auckland. Four able seaman ratings were killed and another two seriously injured. Then two weeks later on 16th January 1942 the *Monowai* was in action with the Japanese submarine *I-20* off the southern coast of Viti Levu, the main island of Fiji, while escorting the Australian troop ship *Taroona* (4,286/1935). By now she was under the command of Captain G.R. Deverell RN. Both ships had just disembarked troops at Suva. Four torpedoes were fired at the *Monowai* all of

For 81 years until 1976 the Union Steam Ship Company operated an overnight service between the ports of Lyttelton in the South Island of New Zealand and Wellington in the North Island. They built a succession of fast, very well appointed coastal passenger liners with which to maintain this trade. Of all those ships, none became more well liked and better remembered than the *Rangatira* of 1931.

Swift, beautiful and a pleasure to travel aboard, this lovely photo captures the *Rangatira* steaming in Cook Strait early in the Second World War. Her name means 'chief' in the Maori language. During the early war years the *Rangatira*, escorted by HMNZS *Monowai*, was often used for carrying troops. With a top speed of 21.4 knots, a gross register tonnage of 6,152 and accommodation for 936 passengers in two classes, the

Rangatira was fitted with turbo-electric machinery – steam turbines driving alternators which supplied electricity for electric motors coupled to twin propellers – to give quiet running and the high astern power needed for berthing each morning. All her successors had this same type of propulsion. The *Rangatira* lasted until November 1967 when she was broken up in Hong Kong. *[Ian J. Farquhar collection]*

which missed, and there followed a brief exchange of gunfire. The submarine escaped by crash diving. This was the only time HMNZS *Monowai* fired her guns at an enemy vessel.

Change of role

On 16th March 1943 HMNZS *Monowai* arrived at Devonport Naval Base, Auckland for refit. By this stage of the war armed merchant cruisers were being withdrawn from use and converted mostly to troop ships as the threat from submarine attack had become too great. So it was for the *Monowai*. No longer required for service in New Zealand and South Pacific waters, she departed Auckland on 24th April 1943 for England via Panama. Anchoring off Greenock, the place of her construction, on 2nd June 1943, she proceeded to Liverpool the following day. There the ship was de-ammunitioned and on 18th June she paid off as an armed merchant cruiser. Her last Royal Navy commanding officer was Captain T.K. Masterman RN. Most of the ship's crew were posted to the new Colony Class cruiser *Gambia*, about to be commissioned at Liverpool to join the British Pacific Fleet. With just three officers and a handful of men left aboard, the *Monowai* was then handed over to the British Ministry of War Transport.

Now began the *Monowai's* conversion to an assault landing ship. The work was carried out at Glasgow over a period of eight months and involved the transformation of the ship. Her armament, mainmast, hydraulic cranes, lifeboats and davits were all removed. In their place an extensive battery of light AA guns was fitted, along with heavy davits on which were stowed 20 motorised assault landing craft. Made of wood, they were 41½ feet in length, each capable of landing 35 troops with full battle gear, and were powered by 130 horsepower petrol motors driving twin propellers. The *Monowai* could now carry up to 1,800 troops with full equipment. In February 1944, under the command of the Union Steam Ship Company's Captain G.B. Morgan RNR, the *Monowai* sailed from Glasgow in her new role with troops for Egypt and Taranto. J. Billingham was her chief officer, H. Simmonds her chief engineer and B. Hurley the ship's purser. All four men were New Zealanders. Leaving Taranto with Yugoslav refugees aboard, the *Monowai* went to Sicily from where she returned to Liverpool carrying troops and a large shipment of gold bullion. Captain Morgan had been the *Awatea's* final master.

From April 1944 the *Monowai* was based in the Solent, Southampton, preparing for the D-Day landings. Four days prior to the great event on 6th June 1944, Captain Morgan was invalided off the ship

The *Monowai* as an armed merchant cruiser (top and middle right). Splinter mattresses have been fixed to the front of her bridge, the port and starboard wings of which have been cut down for the fitting of searchlights, while the monkey island has become the compass platform, from which the ship was navigated. The *Monowai's* relatively high speed, for a merchant ship, of 19 knots meant she was chosen for this role instead of the non-combatant work of a hospital ship, as was the case with the much slower 14 knot *Wanganella*. From June 1943 to February 1944 the *Monowai* was extensively refitted as an assault landing ship at Glasgow, just as the *Awatea* had been in 1942. The result (below) was a much more potent and convincing ship of war. Her forward well deck has been plated-in, Carley floats are mounted on her foremast rigging and there is a radar installation above the bridge. The starboard-side assault landing craft lie suspended from their davits outboard of what had once been the first and second class promenade decks. For the D-Day invasion ten assault craft were doubled-banked along each side of the ship. Accommodation for 1,800 troops with all their combat gear was built into the *Monowai's* lower decks. *[Both: Ian J. Farquhar collection]* In place of the old six-inch guns the *Monowai's* upper decks are sprinkled with anti-aircraft weaponry: one 4-inch and two 12-pounder AA guns aft, two single 2-pounder AA guns forward of the bridge, two single 44-mm AA guns either side of the fore-funnel, eight single 20-mm AA guns and eight rocket projectors abaft the funnels. The mainmast has been removed to give the AA gunners

unimpaired sky arcs over the stern of the ship. The ten starboard-side assault landing craft lie suspended from their davits outboard of what had once been the first and second class promenade decks. In this view

(below) L51 *Monowai* is off the Isle of Wight for the invasion rehearsal that took place between 24th and 28th April 1944. *[Imperial War Museum A23740]*

After landing 73,000 troops in France during Operation Neptune, *Monowai* was employed repatriating prisoners of war to their home countries following the surrenders of Germany and Japan (above). These voyages took her all over the world. In the photo below she has some 850 British personnel embarked after their release from three and a half years' captivity in Singapore and Malaya. The *Monowai* carried them to Liverpool, which she reached on 8th October 1945. *[Top: Ian J. Farquhar collection, bottom: Imperial War Museum H42234]*

British ex-prisoners of war and internees on their way home from Singapore aboard the *Monowai* (left). A large group of them are gathered around the *Monowai's* number three hatch abaft the liner's bridge, where an embarkation officer is briefing them on the voyage ahead. They have all been nursed back to health after years of near-starvation and brutality at the hands of the Japanese. Note at the top of the picture, two of the heavy davits for the *Monowai's* assault landing craft. *[Imperial War Museum H42235]*

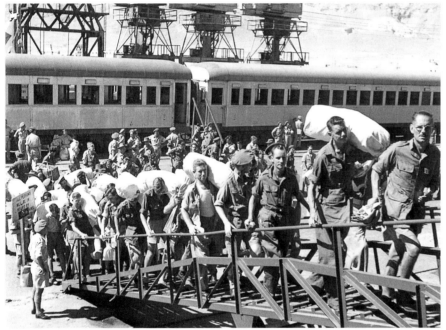

After transiting the Suez Canal on the voyage home to England, the *Monowai* called at the port of Suez for bunkers. Here, the ex-POW service personnel were disembarked from the ship and issued with new uniforms by the British military authorities in Cairo. In this picture (left) they are boarding the *Monowai* with full kit bags after leaving the train that has returned them to the docks. Their next port of call will be Liverpool. Good food and medical care has transformed the men in this photo from walking skeletons at the time when they were liberated from the Japanese. *[Imperial War Museum H42238]*

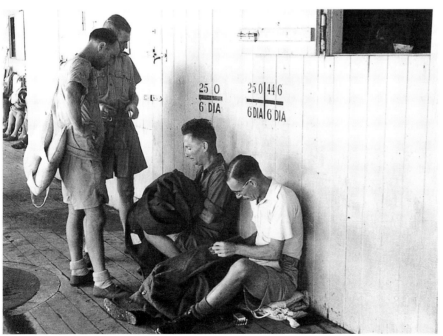

Two men attend to their newly issued kit (left) while sitting on the *Monowai's* promenade deck, sheltered from the hot Mediterranean sun. The man at right, clearly still recovering his body weight after the long ordeal of captivity, is sewing badges of rank on to the sleeves of his uniform shirts. He is wearing new shoes and socks; it will have been over three years since his feet last had such comfort. Beside him, watched by two others (one of whom is carrying his lifejacket) a second man is working on what appears to be his newly-issued army bedroll. *[Imperial War Museum H442239]*

Watched by former POWs in their new uniforms, a child whose name is recorded as Gordon McIntyre is shown (left) playing with toys that have been donated by the British Red Cross. One of many civilians interned in Singapore for the duration of the war, he is seated on top of a wooden life raft in the deck space between the *Monowai's* funnels and her bridge. Behind him is part of the forward boiler room skylight, just ahead of the fore funnel. *[Imperial War Museum H42242]*

Another child internee (left) playing with a rocking horse and toy rabbit on top of the wooden life rafts stacked in the same deck area separating the *Monowai's* funnels and bridge. Looking on are former POWs including two British Army officers at right. The toys were distributed to the children aboard the *Monowai* by Miss Anne Small of the British Red Cross; she is possibly the woman standing in front of the stowed cargo derrick at left. As the UK neared and the ex-POWs began to regain their physical well-being, the mood lightened and their long journey home turned into something of a well-deserved holiday. This would have contrasted sharply with memories of the incessant drill, inspections and war preparation that filled the days aboard the troopships that took these same men out to Singapore in 1941. *[Imperial War Museum 42243]*

The same deck scene (left) as in the above photo, viewed looking down from just under the port AA gun tub abreast the fore-funnel. The boy with the over-large shorts is still on his rocking horse. Behind him, another child is playing with one of the ex-POWs while officers and men look on. Part of the number three hatch can be seen at the top left of the picture, along with part of a steam winch at right. The open doors lead to the deck officers' accommodation in the *Monowai's* bridge island. *[Imperial War Museum 42244]*

and replaced temporarily by Captain W. Whitefield, also from the Union Company and formerly Master of the liner *Aorangi*. For the *Monowai* came the distinction of being in the spearhead of troop ships moving British and Canadian forces to the landings on Normandy's Gold Beach. With 1,800 troops aboard, she left Cowes Roads for Normandy on the evening of 5th June as part of a vast invasion fleet. Disembarkation commenced at 6.15 next morning after an uneventful over-night passage. Throughout the day all her troops went ashore but casualties were very high and only six of the *Monowai's* 20 assault craft survived.

The *Monowai* made 20 return trips between Southampton and the Normandy invasion beaches loaded with troops, followed by 25 further trips to the port of Le Havre. After two weeks in hospital Captain Morgan had resumed command and for 12 months the *Monowai* steamed continuously with only two short dockyard visits for boiler maintenance. She successfully landed some 73,000 troops. The only damage incurred during this magnificent effort was when she was blown against one of the piers while coming alongside at Cherbourg in high winds. On 22nd April 1945 the *Monowai* sailed from Plymouth with 1,610 Soviet ex-prisoners of war, transporting them to Odessa in a convoy with four other Allied troop ships. More voyages were made repatriating POWs to France and the USSR and bringing Indian troops home to Bombay. From there she was sent to Colombo to join the British Pacific Fleet.

On 15th August 1945 the war against Imperial Japan ended. Three weeks later on 8th September the *Monowai* was part of the second merchant ship convoy to arrive at Singapore following the surrender. She then became the first ship to leave Singapore with British POWs embarked, taking some 850 former prisoners and civilians home to England and a huge welcome at Liverpool where she berthed on 8th October 1945. Many further voyages were made repatriating troops and POWs from the Far East to Britain, India and Australia, and it was not until 29th August 1946 that she came back to Sydney badly in need of a refit, her war service over. In total she had transported 105,000 troops, POWs and civilians and steamed 121,000 miles. During her service as an armed merchant cruiser she had steamed 140,000 miles.

Return to the Tasman

The *Monowai* was released to her owner in September 1946. Like all British shipping interests the Union Steam Ship Company's managers now had to resume peacetime operations with old and depleted fleets and little prospect of quick or affordable new building. The nearly-new *Awatea* had been lost in 1942 and the worn-out *Monowai* was now 21-years old. Because of this and particularly because of her fuel-hungry and outdated engines, the Union Company was not keen on retaining the *Monowai*. But the company decided, very wisely as it proved, not to replace either her or the *Awatea* with a new liner but instead to modernise the *Monowai* and place her back on the Australia

No mistaking the location of this view: the *Monowai* passing under the Sydney Harbour Bridge probably at the time of her sea trials in January 1949, following her extensive and very lengthy post-war refit. *[Roy Fenton collection]*

This superb portrait from the collection of Vic Young shows the *Monowai* berthed at Queens Wharf in Wellington, New Zealand, on 9th March 1950. It is just over 13 months since she began her post-war trans-Tasman sailings following her reconstruction at Sydney. Every light on the liner's upper decks, including those inside her wheelhouse, is switched on to render this lovely memory on a warm autumn evening of one of New Zealand's best known ships. *[V.H. Young and L.A. Sawyer]*

to New Zealand passenger service. Mort's Dock and Engineering Co. Ltd. of Sydney was awarded the contract and work began on reconditioning the *Monowai* in October 1946. The Union Company expected to have its ship back on the Tasman Sea by the start of June 1948.

But three weeks later, industrial trouble stopped all further work and the *Monowai* lay idle until 17th February 1947. Work continued but with stoppages and disruption from non-availability of materials and it was not until mid-January 1949 that she ran her sea trials off Sydney. The cost of refurbishing the *Monowai* came to almost £1 million. Departure for her first post-war sailing to Wellington was set for 24th January 1949 just seven weeks after the *Wanganella*, her lengthy repairs completed, had re-entered service.

Sydney-siders who remembered the old *Monowai* from pre-war times found themselves looking at a very different ship. Opinion was not universally in favour of her new appearance. The forward well deck had gone, plated-in during the landing ship conversion in 1943. The mainmast and hydraulic cranes, also removed during the war, had been replaced by twin kingposts and derricks aft plus four new derricks rigged off the foremast. Her twin raked funnels had been enlarged by slicing them open from top to bottom then welding

new plates to alter the funnels' shape from round to elliptical. On the liner's boat deck were six new lifeboats on gravity davits while the A Deck promenade had been partially enclosed with bulwarks and windows. A new varnished teak bridge with curved front had been fitted where the armoured compass platform and wing searchlights had been. Completely new accommodation for 181 first class and 205 cabin class passengers was built, each class having a separate lounge and smoke room on A Deck. The two dining rooms, located on C Deck, provided seating for 124 in first class and 132 in cabin class. All first class cabins were on A and B Decks while cabin class accommodation was aft on B Deck and on C Deck. Her officers and crew numbered 187 and her gross register tonnage had increased from 10,852 to 11,037. Once again the *Monowai* was under the command of her wartime master, 63-year-old Captain G.B. Morgan DSO DSC, who would remain in command until he retired in November 1950.

After an absence of nearly ten years the *Monowai* berthed at Wellington's Queens Wharf on 27th January 1949. Her first trans-Tasman voyage had been without passengers but she was fully booked for her return to Sydney, departing the following day. For the next 11 years the *Monowai* maintained the Tasman service in partnership with the *Wanganella*, crossings taking three and a half days at a speed of 14 knots and

The *Monowai* underway in Auckland Harbour, most likely outbound for Sydney early in the 1950s before radar was fitted to the ship. Note the canvas screens rigged on her boat deck abaft the bridge for the comfort of first class passengers braving the Tasman weather. *[V.H. Young and L.A. Sawyer]*

The *Monowai* on a fine sunny day in Wellington Harbour, getting underway having just left Queens Wharf with passengers for Sydney. In this view her radar tower, added during an early 1950s refit, can be seen on the roof of the bridge. The *Monowai* was not altered significantly during her final decade of service and the fitting of radar was probably the only external change made to her. Mount Victoria with its twin radio masts can be seen on the skyline behind the ship. Also visible in this photo is St Gerard's Monastery in Oriental Bay, just above the stowed derricks aft on the liner's cabin class promenade. *[V.H. Young and L.A. Sawyer]*

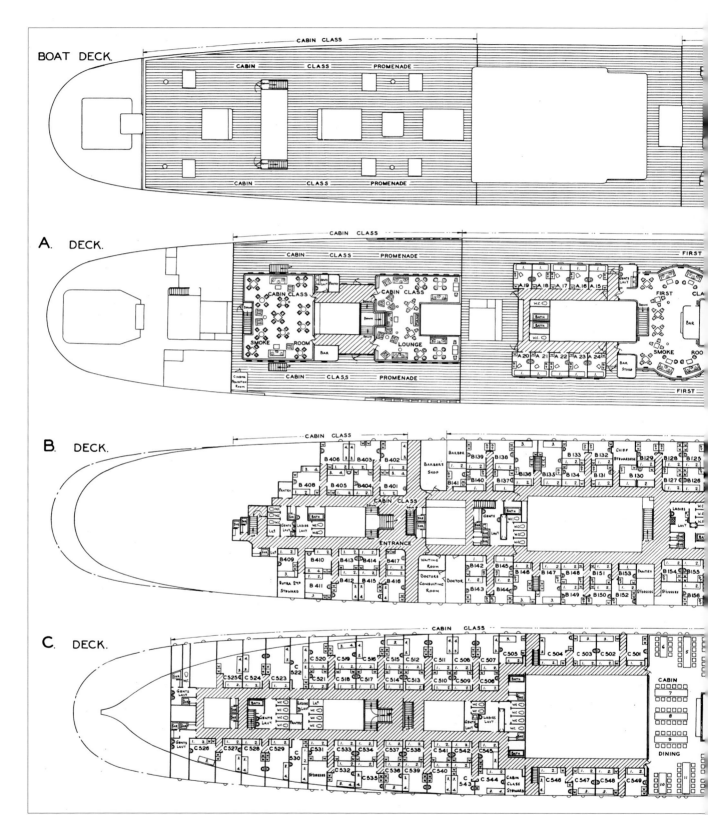

Cabin plan of *Monowai*

There are probably no surviving general arrangement plans of the *Monowai* or the *Razmak*, owing to a lack of publicity from her entry into entry into service being overshadowed by the delivery to P&O of three C class and four R class ships in 1925. This cabin plan is dated 1950 and shows arrangements after the *Monowai* was reconditioned following her Second World War service. *[Andrew Bell collection]*

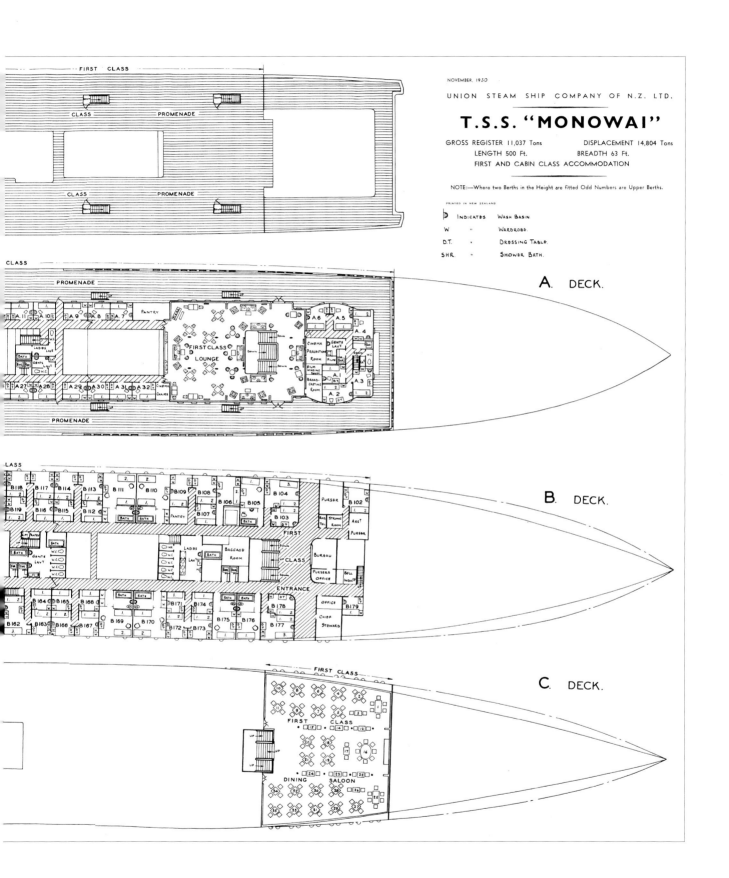

Another shot of the *Monowai* departing Wellington for Sydney at the start of one of her regular Tasman crossings. In this view a strong north-westerly wind is blowing across the harbour and only a handful of passengers have lingered on her boat deck as she moves away from Queens Wharf. *[V.H. Young and L.A. Sawyer]*

This image by Vic Young of the *Monowai* slowly underway in Wellington Harbour captures how different her profile was from that of the *Wanganella*. At 519 feet overall, she was 40 feet longer than the *Wanganella* and her draught fully loaded at 34 feet was almost 10 feet greater. In this view she is probably shifting berth while working cargo between Tasman voyages. *[V.H. Young and L.A. Sawyer]*

alternating between Sydney and Auckland then Sydney and Wellington. She was a familiar sight in all three ports and became immensely popular with the travelling public. During the Christmas holiday peak seasons she would be fully booked, with cabin occupancy for the remainder of the year averaging 75% in 1953. As in pre-war years, summer cruises were made to Milford Sound in Fiordland, New Zealand. Many young officers who went on to command the Union Steam Ship Company's ships in the 1950s and 1960s served aboard the *Monowai*. She was known to be a happy ship. For the entire decade of the 1950s her master was Captain F.W. Young.

In 1951 the *Monowai* was laid up for three months between April and July during a prolonged and bitter waterfront strike. Industrial conflict was a feature of the post-war shipping industry in both Australia and New Zealand. On 11th April 1957, just prior to her departure for Sydney with all passenger cabins filled, newspaper headlines announced that the '*Monowai's* crew refuses to man ship', causing the Union Company to withdraw the liner 'indefinitely' from service. Passenger numbers slowly declined during the mid to late 1950s as air travel grew. Observing this, the Union Company again decided not to replace the *Monowai* but instead, gave her an extensive refit in 1956 that would keep her operational for a further four years. Ironically, in 1959 the *Monowai's* cabin occupancy grew to 85% and during the peak summer season she was fully booked for most trans-Tasman voyages.

The *Monowai* turns to present her counter stern as she leaves her berth at Wellington. The nor'westerly is whipping smoke away from the crew galley flue, while the liner's Second Officer keeps watch at her stern rail. The deck crowd, having let go the stern ropes a few minutes earlier, have already vanished below decks out of the wind. *[V.H. Young and L.A. Sawyer]*

Farewell *Monowai*

But in the face of air competition there was no future in the trans-Tasman passenger trade. On 11th November 1959 the Head Office of the Union Company in Wellington announced that she was to be withdrawn at the end of May 1960 and the trans-Tasman service left to the *Wanganella*. She was not to be replaced, evoking much criticism from the local tourist and travel industry. On 27th May 1960 the *Monowai* sailed from Sydney for her final Tasman crossing, bid farewell by a crowd of thousands and with the sirens of nearby ships blaring in salute. She arrived in Auckland on 31st May. Two days later on Thursday 2nd June she left Auckland on a Pacific Island cruise that, over the next 18 days, took her to ports in Tonga, Samoa and Fiji where she had become so well known during the 1930s and during her time

as an armed merchant cruiser. Fares for the cruise started from £100. On returning to Auckland on Sunday 19th June 1960 the *Monowai* disembarked her very last passengers, then at 10.00 pm left for Wellington after a farewell reunion of former war-time crew members had been held aboard the liner. After a two-day voyage down the east coast of the North Island, the old ship berthed at Clyde Quay Wharf in Wellington at 10.40 am on 22nd June. Over the course of the next few days she was stripped of stores and furnishings, Captain Young left the ship and her remaining crew members were paid off. The last to leave was her carpenter W. Hendry, who had been with the *Monowai* since she resumed peacetime sailings in 1949.

Earlier in June 1960 it had been reported that the Union Company had sold the *Monowai* for £165,000. Her new owner was the Far East Metal Industries and Shipping Company of Hong Kong, who intended to demolish the ship for her steel. She remained at Clyde Quay Wharf for the next six and a

These two superb photos, one to port (left) and the other to starboard (right) look astern across the boat deck and funnels of the *Monowai* at sea. Note how beautifully she was maintained by her crew; only the two fire buckets in the starboard view are out of place.

The *Monowai's* foredeck with the ship's foremast and cargo gear for numbers one and two holds (above left). This photo was taken from the liner's bridge. Note the steam winch at left foreground, the winch operator's cabs with their windows and open doors and the raised derricks, each with a lifting capacity of five tons, their heels mounted against the trunks for the big exhaust vents on either side of the mast.

A scene doubtless fixed in the memories of countless passengers and ships' crews arriving at or leaving Sydney: the *Monowai* approaching Sydney's mighty harbour bridge and about to run beneath it (above right). *[All: V.A Young and L.A. Sawyer]*

Aboard the *Monowai* at sea in 1953, looking across the port accident boat and the foredeck from the forward observation deck under the port wing of the bridge.

As she'll always be remembered, the *Monowai* shows off her best angle in this photo, taken in Wellington Harbour. Her long, low profile made her unique when compared to the towering P&O, Orient and Shaw Savill liners that often were berthed nearby when she was in port. *[Ian J. Farquhar collection]*

The *Monowai* on the afternoon of 16th August 1960 at the very end of her long life, steaming out of Wellington Harbour for the final time. Her new owners have added a narrow white band to each of her funnels. Passing the liner on her port bow is the Wellington Harbour Board's grab hopper dredge *Kerimoana*. The large rocks in the middle distance are those to seaward of Pencarrow Head, on the eastern side of the harbour entrance channel. *[Alexander Turnbull Library, Wellington, New Zealand. Dominion Post Collection, EP/1960/2956/9]*

half weeks. On 15th August smoke was seen emerging from her funnels, to which single white bands had been added, as preparations were made for her final departure. Her Master for this last voyage was Captain S.M. Barling, her Chief Engineer F.G. Sewell of Hong Kong, and J.A. Brown was her Chief Officer. The crew comprised some 50 Chinese and Europeans.

In rain showers and a stiff north-westerly breeze the *Monowai's* head and stern ropes were let go at 3pm on Tuesday 16th August 1960. Captain G.H. Edwards, the Union Company's Assistant Marine Superintendent, was the last off the ship. Slowly she moved away from Clyde Quay Wharf watched by a sombre gathering of former crew members many of whom were seen to remove their hats. Three short blasts on her steam whistles were answered by other ships berthed in Wellington. Making black smoke the *Monowai* steamed slowly round the harbour and out through the entrance. Turning westwards into the Tasman Sea for the very last time, she was on her way to Hong Kong where landfall was made on 6th

September. A week later on 13th September she was towed across Kowloon Bay for scrapping.

In a sad postscript to the life of the *Monowai*, an auction of fittings and furnishings removed from the liner was held on 6th September 1960 at a public venue in Wellington known as the Winter Show Buildings. Up to one thousand prospective bidders were in attendance as all the cabin and lounge furniture from the *Monowai* was sold. Such was the attachment to the ship that many people sought out familiar items from particular cabins that they had occupied on innumerable crossings. Fifteen years later, in honour of her war service, the *Monowai's* name was given to the Royal New Zealand Navy's newly acquired survey ship which commissioned on 1st July 1975.

The Union Steam Ship Company's 123 years of shipping trade on the Tasman Sea came to an end in 1999. The company was notable for fine ships that gave long and dependable service. Of all of them, the 30-year achievement of the *Monowai* in war and peace must rank among the more meritorious.

Last voyage. The *Monowai* calling at Brisbane for bunkers on 20th August 1960, having just crossed the Tasman Sea four days after she left Wellington. It is two months since her very last passengers disembarked yet the ship looks as tidily maintained as she always was. In seventeen days she will make Hong Kong and 'finished with engines' will be rung down from her bridge for the last time. Scrapping commenced three and a half weeks after this photo was taken. Note the thin white bands her new owners the Far East Metal Industries and Shipping Company have painted on her funnels. *[V.H. Young and L.A. Sawyer]*

INDEX

Ships' names are in italics
The place names of Auckland, Australia,
England, New Zealand, Sydney,
Tasman, Tasman Sea, trans-Tasman
and Wellington all of which occur
throughout the book, are not listed.

The *Monowai* underway in Sydney Harbour prior to the Second World War, photographed from the Sydney Harbour Bridge. She is outward bound with Sydney Cove or Circular Quay, as it is also known, behind her. The wharves at upper left have all gone, as has the tram depot which is just out of the picture at left. The Sydney Opera House and its approaches are now located where they once stood. Jack Churchouse, founding Curator of the Wellington Maritime Museum in New Zealand, always considered the *Monowai* to have had a much more pleasing profile as she was during her pre-war years. A great friend to shipping artists, writers and photographers, Jack Churchouse served as a junior deck officer aboard the *Monowai* during the 1950s before moving to the Port Line. He died in 1993.
[Ian J. Farquhar collection]

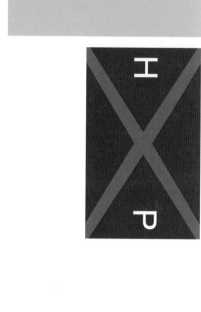

Huddart Parker Limited

Hang Fung Shipping and Trading Company Limited

McIlwraith, McEacharn Limited

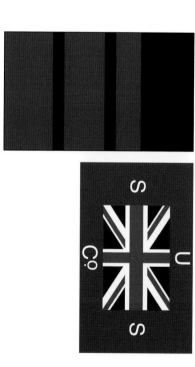

Union Steam Ship Company of New Zealand Limited